Going 15 Rounds With Jerry Izenberg

Ed Odeven

Published by Ed Odeven, 2020.

Going 15 Rounds With Jerry Izenberg
A Collection Of Interviews With The Legendary Columnist
Ed Odeven
Published by Ed Odeven, 2020.

GOING 15 ROUNDS WITH JERRY IZENBERG

First edition. December 31, 2020.

Copyright © 2020 Ed Odeven.

ISBN: 978-1393156055

Written by Ed Odeven.

GOING 15 ROUNDS WITH JERRY IZENBERG

First edition. December 31, 2020.

Copyright © 2020 Ed Odeven.

ISBN: 978-1393156055

Written by Ed Odeven.

Table Of Contents

Introduction

This isn't just a Q&A anthology, a long-form interview project featuring Jerry Izenberg. There's much more to share.

To tell his story, to highlight various facets of his life's work, it was important to reach out to dozens of people who've known Jerry and been familiar with his work. In some cases, this stretches back decades (including the late Dave Anderson, Jerry Green, Dave Kindred, John Schulian and Ira Berkow) while other distinguished sources (such as Jeremy Schaap, Wallace Matthews, Kevin Iole and Tom Verducci) gained appreciation for Izenberg's newspaper gravitas, storytelling skills and sports knowledge later on.

This portion of the book shares insights from several dozen individuals who've formed opinions about Jerry's columns, his approach to writing, his passion for telling stories, his lifelong commitment to the craft.

Pick a place, any place, and Izenberg has probably stepped foot into the joint and observed mankind's competitive fire within the boundaries of the building, or watched up close in American stadiums from coast to coast and during overseas reporting excursions.

In press boxes, boxing gyms, horse tracks, overseas sports venues, restaurants, TV studios, taxi cabs and elsewhere, Part II's cast of characters has watched Izenberg go about his work and then seen the finished product: polished, thought-provoking columns about an endless array of topics. Columns were always the hallmark of his career, of course, but they've watched the TV appearances, heard the delightful sarcasm and rapid-fire knowledge of sports history on the radio and recognized the value of what he brought to the business.

Anecdotal tales of Jerry's career fill the pages of Part II. What's more, impressions of how and why he became one of the legends of American sports media are told again and again.

One year, in particular, is a culmination of all those stories.

In 2000, Izenberg received The Associated Press Sports Editors' Red Smith Award, which is the highest honor given to a print journalist by the organization. In 2000, he was also inducted into the National Sportscasters and Sportswriters Association Hall of Fame (now known as the National Sports Media Association).

Writers rave about Izenberg's never-wavering dedication, his precision in making a point, his unbridled enthusiasm for delivering a message in print and online, even as he approached his 90th birthday on September 10, 2020.

Broadcasters, too, expressed awe in his ability to stay fired up for the game, for championship week, for marquee fights, and for remaining true to his roots every step of the way.

In the section that follows, Izenberg's peers explain why he's a quintessential "old school newspaperman." Others described him as an icon, a gifted pundit, a New Jersey legend, someone who is part of the Mount Rushmore of great sports journalists.

Personal memories from renowned journalists and broadcasters Robert Lipsyte, George Solomon, Bill Dwyre, Charley Steiner, Mark Whicker, Jim Lampley, Dave Sims and Ivan Maisel, among others, reflect on Jerry's long list of accomplishments. Admirers and critics, they and their contemporaries shine light on what's made Izenberg so good—and so relevant—for so long.

***

Starting in the fall of 2015, research, interviews and revisions were done over the next several years.

There were times when the project was on hold for several weeks or months and little progress was made, but motivation was always there to keep focused on the task at hand. For me, though, this was one of those ah-ha moments that sparked interest in this project: In the days and weeks after Muhammad Ali's passing in June 2016, Izenberg's remarkable memory and gift for storytelling enriched our understanding of The Greatest's special place as a sports figure and global icon.

On radio and TV appearances, we were reminded once again of Izenberg's unique place in sports journalism in the 20th and 21st centuries.

His sustained excellence as a journalist has bridged the gap from the old school to the current era, with generations of readers learning the real stories behind the stories.

In 2019, Izenberg, then 89, completed his first novel. It's a testament to his never-wavering commitment to his craft. Writing matters greatly to him. Telling stories is a gift that he's shared with readers for decades.

The new book is called "After the Fire." Izenberg, who was inducted into the New Jersey Hall of Fame in the same year, explained the project this way: "(It) is set in Newark, N.J., 1967-68 during and after the Newark Riot (26 dead) and the struggle between the Italians and the Afro-Americans for political control of the city in the wake of what was the first in a chain of civil explosions that long hot summer.

"I grew up in that city. It is where I went to college and where I lived and worked. Like our entire staff I helped cover that riot. Newark is the home of The Star-Ledger to which I returned in 1962 after (four) years at the New York Herald Tribune. It is a city whose neighborhoods I walked and whose people I know and whose urban changes I witnessed.

"The book's plot is centered around a mayoral election steeped in the emotional wake of the riot, three very real and prominent mafiosos who attempt to fix it—Richie 'The Boot' Boiardo, (Genovese Family), Carlo Gambino (the family of the same name) and Frank Costello (tied to Gambino). They inject a celebrity into the mix—a Jersey-born singer named Frank Sinatra.

"The trio of candidates who fuel and feed off the city-wide tensions are the Italo-American who founded the local White Citizens Council in the city's North Ward, a charismatic Afro-American, who has captured the loyalty of the heavily Afro-American Central Ward, and an outsider who is also black, very wealthy and connected with the city's financial power structure.

"Against that backdrop of fear, hate and insular desperation, a single ray of hope emerges as a continuing theme—the love affair between a black college girl and an Italian college boy. In the Newark of 1967-68, they meet in the only place in the city that year where they could—the main post office with summer jobs.

"In what this Northern blue-collar town became back then they can't even walk down the street holding hands. They date in secret. But, once revealed, their relationship impacts with every group and every set of parents in what that Newark had become."

The wide world of sports, of course, is the big canvas on which Izenberg's words painted vivid pictures about games, personalities and notable subjects, and they'll be explored in the pages that follow.

Foreword

Jerry Izenberg's newspaper career began in 1951 in a vastly different era. New York City was still home to three Major League Baseball teams (the Yankees, Giants and Dodgers), and it was in the middle of a golden era for baseball in the big city.

Izenberg started working for The Star-Ledger in his hometown of as a copy boy. He also gained experience as a sports reporter for the Observer, the Rutgers-Newark student newspaper.

When he was a college junior, he began working with his lifelong colleague Sid Dorfman, who passed away in February 2014.

Sixty-plus years after Dorfman served as his first boss, Jerry paid tribute to him in a column. Izenberg's mentor left an indelible mark on his life.

"To all of us, Sid Dorfman was the final arbiter on all things sports," Izenberg wrote. "I am 83 years old and I cannot remember or even picture The Star-Ledger without Sid. All I know of its history begins with Sid.

"I worked for him as a college kid at The Star-Ledger when he was the slot man (night copy desk editor) and at his major operation called Dorf Feature Service that began as a clearinghouse for high school sports scores and ultimately serviced the paper with suburban municipal meetings from the sewer commissions to the city councils and the boards of education."

After serving in the U.S. Army during the Korean War, Izenberg relaunched his career as a newspaperman. He worked for weekly newspapers. He paid the bills with a stint at the Paterson News, then moved to the New York Herald Tribune before returning to The Star-Ledger as a sports columnist, a full-time gig until 2009, when he scaled back his workload to so-called semi-retired status.

***

Decade after decade, Izenberg delivered the goods. His sustained excellence as a sports writer, especially as a columnist, covers many subjects: the NFL and baseball, boxing and horse racing to name a few.

In October 2019, Izenberg was inducted into the New Jersey Hall of Fame, the 16th Hall of Fame to enshrine him. Indeed, no small feat.

"It didn't take me long to understand the value of a New Jersey upbringing," Izenberg told The Star-Ledger in June 2019 for a story carrying the announcement of the 2019 inductees. "At 5:10 on a Sunday night, in Newark's Beth Israel Hospital, a doctor slapped me on the ass and said, 'You're in New Jersey, kid. Go figure out how to survive.' "

Izenberg survived and thrived in his chosen profession.

His memoir, "Through My Eyes: A Sports Writer's 58-Year Journey," was published in 2009.

That didn't signal the end of his career. It was simply one more milestone for the man born on Sept. 10, 1930, at Newark's Beth Israel Hospital.

Izenberg keeps churning out columns for The Star-Ledger, crafting one-of-a-kind remembrances of sporting legends who've passed away and memorable dispatches on Triple Crown horse races, Super Bowls and boxing fights and the run-up to these marquee events.

Simply put, being semi-retired isn't a phrase that does justice to Jerry Izenberg.

"I've got to do something because it's what I do," he said in a 2017 interview.

Writing authoritative books about boxing, for instance.

"The Golden Era of Heavyweight Boxing," which covers the period from 1962 to 1997, reaffirmed Izenberg's reputation as a deeply knowledgeable chronicler of the sweet science. One of the true insiders of the sport, his status as a boxing historian cannot be disputed.

Positive reviews of the book, which was published in February 2017, followed.

"Jerry Izenberg has written the most accurate and entertaining boxing book I have ever read," trainer Freddie Roach declared.

Writer John Schulian presented this viewpoint: "Once There Were Giants is a history lesson that dances the way Ali did and packs the wallop of Frazier's left hook. Only Jerry Izenberg, with sixty-plus years of no-BS reporting and bristling prose behind him, could have brought back to life the greatest era boxing's heavyweights ever saw. He knew the fighters from Liston and Foreman to Holmes and Tyson, and he had a pipeline to the mob guys, corner men, TV executives, and flimflamming promoters. There isn't another sportswriter in America who's been at ringside so long or tells the stories he found there so memorably."

USA Today's review stated: "An extraordinary, historically accurate chronicle of the golden era of heavyweight boxing in the U.S. ... one of those gems you can't put down once you start reading."

***

An irreplaceable trademark of Izenberg's career was his run of Super Bowls, from the first one in 1967 (at the Los Angeles Memorial Coliseum) until Super Bowl LIII in 2019 (at Mercedes-Benz Stadium in Atlanta).

In ending The Streak in 2020, Izenberg used his column to explain why he made that decision. (And it left Jerry Green of the Detroit News as the only newspaper columnist to attend every Super Bowl.)

"I'm old, not dead," Izenberg wrote, while later admitting it's a struggle for his 89-year-old legs to navigate large crowds and pound the pavement for long distances.

He prefaced that sentence by looking back at his long run of covering every pro gridiron title match since the Eisenhower administration.

"Fifty-three years," Izenberg wrote. "That's how long Part 2 of my pro football seasons always ended with the Super Bowl, a game whose name sounded like a breakfast cereal. Before that, from 1957 to 1966, there was a decade of NFL and AFL championship games, and I wrote about all of them, too—until now.

"This year, the streak will end. I won't be at Super Bowl 54 in Miami.

"As I told Bill Vinovich, who will be the referee on Feb. 2, when the San Francisco 49ers meet the Kansas City Chiefs: 'Flip the coin. You can start without me. It's time to get off stage.' "

From his Nevada home, Izenberg wrote columns in the run-up to Super Bowl LIV, sharing memories of past games, colorful personalities and moments from Super Bowl week.

For his Super Bowl Sunday column, he predicted the correct final score: Chiefs 31, 49ers 20.

Associated Press writer Tim Dahlberg's column about Izenberg in the run-up to the Super Bowl wrapped up this way: "His friends are mostly all gone now, and his membership in a rare club is about to come to an end, like it has for all of them. Izenberg will watch this Super Bowl from the comfort of the sports book at the Sunset Station.

"He will, of course, write a column about the degenerate gamblers and what they thought of the game. Because while he may not be in Miami, a good writer never really quits."

An Appraisal

How four columns spanning decades provides a meaningful introduction to Jerry Izenberg's work.

1. On Junius Kellogg

In June 1965, Jerry Izenberg penned a column on former college basketball player Junius Kellogg, who was paralyzed 11 years earlier in a car accident.

In the early years of his gig as a columnist, there were clear signs that Jerry was in his element.

The column didn't dwell on the life-changing aspect of Kellogg's life, but showed how dignity and pride are central themes in his life. Without preaching, Izenberg also urged the public to support wheelchair athletes.

In slightly under 1,000 words, Izenberg's column accomplished a lot.

It's a revealing portrait of Izenberg's career, a glimpse at his ability to find and tell compelling stories anywhere.

Decades later, longtime New York metropolitan region sportswriter Filip Bondy said that he remembered reading about Kellogg and caring about the story because Jerry cared about it.

"Junius Kellogg was a forgotten hero, and Jerry deserves credit for bringing him back to light," Bondy remarked in an interview. "That inspired me to meet Junius and write several stories about him. Jerry was a great advocate for Junius, who needed one. Unfortunately, the Basketball Hall of Fame failed to elect Junius, though he was a finalist."

Here's the opening of Izenberg's column:

"It was a great fight. All through the game Tony Mucci and Danny Vacarro had been jabbing elbows at each other and finally there were some words and one guy said, 'If you do that again I'll hand you your head' and the other guy did it.

" 'That's when I looked up from the bench,' " Junius Kellogg said, 'and I saw these two wheelchairs heading straight for each other at top speed and they banged together and everyone was pushing and shoving and knocking chairs together. Then Tony's wife came out of the crowd and she started to swing her pocketbook.

" 'Man it was wild.'

"The thing happened a couple of years ago between the Pan-Am Jets and the Brooklyn Whirlaways, a couple of wheelchair basketball teams. The people who play this game have been in hospitals where they learned they could never walk again or where their necks were in traction or where they could have looked up at the ceiling day after day and said, 'Why me?' and given the whole thing up.

"But sing no sad songs for baby. All they want is a chance to work and a set of good wheels and, if anything, they attack life a little harder. They work harder and they play harder and mostly it's because they have done a lot of hard thinking."

Junius Kellogg died in September 1998 at age 71.

By that time, and in the years since then, many people may have forgotten what happened to him during his sophomore year at Manhattan College, where he was the school's first black scholarship athlete.

What eventually was brought into the open was a point-shaving scandal of epic proportions: 32 players from seven colleges eventually admitted to accepting bribes.

How big was it? It involved 86 games in 17 states between 1947 and 1950, according to Kellogg's obituary in The New York Times.

Kellogg declined to participate.

The New York Times obit chronicled the incident that triggered law enforcement's involvement.

Manhattan teammate Henry Poppe approached Kellogg in his dormitory room seeking a favor.

"DePaul University was coming to the Garden as a 3-point favorite over Manhattan," the newspaper reported. "Poppe wanted Kellogg, Manhattan's leading scorer, to be sure his team lost by at least 5 or 6 points."

What would've been the payout? A thousand dollars.

"I told him to get the hell out of my room," said Kellogg, who later became a Harlem Globetrotter and was traveling with the team when he became paralyzed.

Dealing with insomnia that night, Kellogg was compelled to discuss the issue with Manhattan coach Kenny Norton, who told him to visit the District Attorney's Office, according to The Times.

"I didn't want to hurt the guy," Kellogg said of Poppe, "but I had to do it. If at any time in the future that guy decided to tell someone he came to see me, my scholarship was gone."

That, of course, wasn't the end of the story.

"The gamblers approached Kellogg again," The Times reported, "and the District Attorney's staff wired him for a listening device to wear when he met the gamblers at a neighborhood bar.

"The gamblers told him to 'throw hook shots over the basket' and 'miss rebounds occasionally,' Kellogg declined, and Manhattan won the game, 62-59. Hours later, the police made the first arrests."

***

After leading the Pan-Am Jets to four international titles in wheelchair basketball between 1957 and '66, he began working as the first deputy commissioner and director of strategic planning for New York City's Community Development Agency.

Stylistically and factually, Izenberg's column packed a potent punch.

The location? The ninth annual United States Wheelchair Games in Jackson Heights, Queens, New York City.

"The competitors—275 of them—are marvelously talented people," Izenberg wrote. "There is not nearly enough money to keep this thing going and to establish facilities for all the people who want to compete and Kellogg thinks that maybe somebody ought to do something about that."

As cited above in his obituary in The New York Times, Kellogg overcame great odds to have a semblance of a normal life, and Izenberg closed out the column by connecting Kellogg's story with a broader theme about disabled athletes—and reminding people to support them.

Izenberg also made sure to inform everyone that Kellogg was a man of strong morals.

"In 1951, a guy named Hank Poppe walked (up) to Kellogg and told him how he could make 10 100-dollar bills by missing baskets," Izenberg wrote. "Junius was a sophomore at Manhattan College and he blew the loudest damn whistle anybody had ever heard and he taught a great many smart guys never to take anything for granted."

He also highlighted Kellogg's hospital recovery and what his life was like in 1965.

"It took Kellogg five years and two hospitals to come back," Izenberg wrote. "He never once thought i would be otherwise. Now he is married and he is doing some writing and he has the bar and grill. He thinks that more people should be concerned about giving the wheelchair athletes a chance to compete.

"He has coached them and he has seen what it can do for a man's spirit.

" 'Tell the people,' he said, 'they can help by sending contributions to Benjamin Upton at the Bulova School of Watchmaking, 4024 62nd St., Woodside, New York.'

"To people who have never had to call themselves gimps and make jokes about the people they call 'good-leggers' it is a very small sacrifice."

Honestly, that was the ideal conclusion for the column.

In other words, Izenberg convinced people to care about wheelchair athletes. It was a very progressive viewpoint.

In 1965, this wasn't your typical sports column topic. But it was a thoughtful piece that discussed athletes, described their games and explained the obstacles they face.

***

David Davis' book, "Wheels of Courage," explores the origin of sports for people with disabilities, including the origins of the Paralympics, which began in 1960. In the book, Davis cites the aforementioned column and Kellogg.

It's a fitting tribute to Izenberg 55 years after his poignant column from the United States Wheelchair Games.

2. On boxing governing bodies (circa January 1971)

Jerry Izenberg packs his columnists with energy and rapid-fire observations, Scene-setting and imagery give the reader a clear idea of what he's talking about.

For instance, a January 1971 column that appeared in The Star-Ledger and was syndicated around the country.

Boxers Bob Foster and Joe Frazier are the featured fighters at the outset of this piece, which appeared in the Lincoln (Nebraska) Evening Journal under this headline: "Light Heavyweight King Foster Flattened by WBA Punch."

"The hardest one-punch fighter in the world today is a light heavyweight named Bob Foster," Izenberg wrote. "In Detroit last year, he hit Joe Frazier smack on the potato and Frazier admits he has never been hit that hard by anything this side of an automatic punch press. But Robert was a light heavyweight trying to do a heavyweight's job, and as always happens in such cases when the heavyweight is a world champion, the light heavyweight comes up short."

Frazier improved to 26-0, knocking out Foster twice in the second round to end it on Nov. 8, 1970.

The facts dictated the column's main points.

"But he is a professional of consummate skills," Izenberg wrote of Foster, "and on the day he went out to fight Joe Frazier he was still the light heavyweight champion of the world.

"The World Boxing Association says he no longer holds that title. He hasn't been hit by anyone since that night in Detroit."

That fight served as the appetizer for a broader commentary that Izenberg made about the WBA and its, as he viewed it, strange machinations.

"When Bob Foster signed to fight Joe Frazier for the heavyweight championship, he agreed to sign to fight a contender named Jimmy Dupree within 90 days," Izenberg wrote. "Those 90 days are up in mid-February. For the benefit of the WBA, which seems to operate on a bent hour-glass, February follows January, the month we are now in.

"In any event, the WBA first took Foster's title away and then realized how absurd that was even for them, so it changed its wording to read that it had withdrawn recognitions—whatever that means."

Bigger stakes, of course, awaited Frazier. The Fight of the Century against Muhammad Ali on March 8, 1971 in New York.

3. On the fate of the USFL

In an April 1984 column ("Fall schedule would spell doom for USFL"), Izenberg correctly predicted that the USFL's interest in switching from a spring to an autumn schedule would be the nail in the coffin for the fledgling circuit.

In clear, hard-hitting prose, he pointed out that the USFL's attendance figures could not sustain the league's economic health.

"This past weekend, it is interesting to note that despite the appearance of football's 40 Million Dollar Man, Steve Young, Los Angeles drew just 10,049 at home," Izenberg noted. "Elsewhere among the league's more significant attendance figures, Washington packed RFK Stadium with 6,075 and the expansion franchise up in Pittsburgh of which the league had spoken so glowingly drew fewer than 17,000 for its game against Denver."

Troubling, indeed.

"The USFL has moved totally away from the master plan with which it might well have proven a lot of so-called smart people wrong," Izenberg wrote.

Izenberg lambasted New Jersey Generals owner Donald Trump's obsession with competing against the NFL, a powerful entity then and even more so now.

"Donald Trump did not buy the Generals to hide them away from the kind of attention New York's beautiful people can shower on a friend who owns a football team," he wrote. "He already speaks about wanting to play the Giants in a big showdown game for charity and he will tell you that there is no football quite like USFL football—a proposition that may be right for all the wrong reasons.

"And then there is television. This is a very dangerous two-edged sword and should be kept out of the hands of children. The men who own the USFL envision a brave new world of autumn where television will carry the day for it. This is a dangerous gamble to say the least. Pro hockey does not have a national commercial network contract. Neither does pro basketball, except for its playoffs.

"As things stand now, if you are addicted to the point where you must see football in the spring, then you do indeed have the USFL—and it has you. But head-to-head in the autumn, if you want football, well, it's there and it's thriving. You do not have to go out and spin the dial to look for it.

"In parting, therefore, let us turn to the words of Chet Simmons, who is no dummy, who holds this league together as commissioner and who well may be about to suffer whiplash when the tail starts to wag this particular dog with more authority.

" 'I'm very pleased with our first year,' he said a few months back. 'We've proved there is room for springtime football.'

"They did—just barely."

The USFL's 1985 season was held in the fall, and that marked the end of the financially strapped league's existence.

4. On Colin Kaepernick

It's 2020, and Izenberg hasn't lost his fastball. Holding powerful people to scrutiny is an important element of his life's work.

For instance, in the aftermath of George Floyd's death, which was caused by police brutality, he revisits the NFL's blackballing of Colin Kaepernick.

Izenberg held nothing back in his critique of NFL commissioner Roger Goodell and the league's handling of the issue.

The June column ("Roger Goodell still owes Colin Kaepernick an apology") packed a punch from the get-go.

Here's how it began:

"We, the NFL, condemn racism and the systematic oppression of Black People. We, the NFL, admit we were wrong for not listening to NFL players earlier and encourage all to speak out and peacefully protest. We, the NFL, believe Black Lives Matter." - Roger Goodell

"Thus did the commissioner of the National Football League join the 21st Century. What delayed his arrival was not prejudice or even conviction. It was simply business as usual, influenced by the collected, banal, midnight tweets of Donald J. Trump. When the President speaks, until now, the league always kowtowed.

"But this past week, in a video that went viral, the players spoke in unison and volume. Without them, there is no product. They were eloquent, unified—and Goodell finally got their message. His decision was strictly business.

"In his 'apology,' Goodell never mentioned Colin Kaepernick. Ignoring Kaepernick's role is like saying Hurricane Katrina was started by a leaky shower in New Iberia, La. Goodell said the league was wrong for not listening to the players. But he avoided apologizing to the man to whom they did listen; the man blackballed by the owners, who, in desperate need of backup quarterbacks, still ostracized him; the man who paid the price for taking on the Establishment.

"They made a farce out of their alleged offer to watch him work out in his attempt to return to his profession.

"One suspects Goodell's earlier position was the direct result of the President's tweet:

" 'Wouldn't you love to see one of the NFL owners, when somebody disrespects our flag, say, 'Get the son of a bitch off the field right now. Out. He's fired. He's fired.' "

Chapter 1: Influences

Jerry Izenberg's one-of-a-kind newspaper career has produced millions of words and countless memorable columns. Since it began in 1951, he's probably seen more sporting events than only a handful of others who've ever worked in the business.

In 2015, just months after witnessing American Pharoah complete his Triple Crown conquest in the Belmont Stakes that June, Izenberg was preparing to write columns from the Breeders' Cup in Kentucky.

Looking back on his epic career, which includes every Super Bowl until the February 2020 game, plus decades of Major League Baseball and Olympic Games, college football and basketball, prizefights and other famous and not-so-famous competitions, and those who've influenced him, Izenberg spoke at length about what he's experienced. He also discussed what's kept him busy in recent years when he's not filing columns for The Newark Star-Ledger.

For instance, putting the finishing touches on "Once They Were Giants," a boxing book released in 2017.

"It's about an era which I consider to be the greatest heavyweight era of all time, because I lived it," Izenberg said. "It starts with Sonny (Liston) knocking out Floyd (Patterson) and it ends with (Mike) Tyson biting (Evander) Holyfield's ear. And there are several others who didn't win championships in the book, but they would certainly be champions today. And, for example Earnie Shavers, who never won a title, was the greatest one-punch champion of a fighter in the division. ...

"The book covers the mob's influence going way back to Owney Madden and Primo Carnera and ends with Frankie Carbo and Blinky Palermo in prison.

"I knew a lot of those guys. ... The anecdotal material in the book is anecdotal material that nobody else ever told."

What sparked his interest in writing this book after completing a biography on former NFL Commissioner Pete Rozelle?

"I just felt it was an era that should not be forgotten, and it's also part of my life," Izenberg said. "Before the Rozelle book, I had finished my autobiography so there was some general (material in there) ... and I also began to realize how well I knew them all personally as friends or not friends. Mike Tyson put his head on my chest and cried, and that's in the book."

In recent years, he's also worked on a novel about black baseball, which had a profound impact on his life as a youngster in Newark, New Jersey.

"I knew so many of those guys because there was a Negro National League team (Newark Eagles) in Newark, and later I covered Monte Irvin and Larry Doby, who came out of that league," said Izenberg, who delivered the eulogy at Doby's funeral in 2003.

***

After entering the newspaper business decades earlier, Izenberg can speak with authority about different eras.

He can provide definitive comparisons between then and now, too.

Izenberg spoke about his days covering baseball, traveling by train with fellow journalists and MLB teams, when the furthest western city was St. Louis and players' salaries weren't astronomically larger than the average American's.

"I remember when Phil Rizzuto and Yogi Berra and Roger Maris came to a place in Newark called the American Shops, it was a men's haberdashery store, and they would spend Saturdays there signing autographs, and the American Shops paid them off in suits," he said. "Well, it shows you how much ballplayers were making. Or how little.

"Everybody had winter jobs," he pointed out, referring to major leaguers. "Nobody could live off what they made. So we had much more common ground with them.

"But then everything changed and they began to make the real shameful sums of money and they had no use for us, and television came in, and not that they were courting the television guys all the time. So everything changed. My relationship with most of them changed. That's my early baseball career."

Asked to reflect on the influence on the journalists and writers who had a profound impact on his career, Izenberg talked about a number of giants in the field, highlighting what he learned from them and how he views their legacies today.

On Ernest Hemingway (1899-1961): Writing short, declarative sentences was a valuable lesson from Papa's work, something Izenberg later tried to impart to his students, including when he taught at The New School for Social Research in New York.

"Somebody gave me like a 110-word sentence," he recalled. "And I said, 'Listen, the Bible says God created the Earth in one day.' "

Simple. And to the point.

"Ernest Hemingway understood that the reputation of words (can be effective), which every English teacher will tell you you can't do, but that's why they are teaching English and not doing it," he said.

"Ernest Hemingway wrote a book called "The Sun Also Rises,' and this is the way one paragraph begins:

'It was a nice day. It was a very nice day. It was a very nice day for fishing.'

"Well that to me was genius. He really told you so much by re-emphasis. ...

"Hemingway was a major influence on me, as far as authors who wrote, not sportswriters."

Who else?

Nelson Algren (1909-81), whose writings on the Southside of Chicago had Izenberg's full, undivided attention.

Algren penned "The Man with the Golden Arm," which won a National Book Award.

"His attention to detail was very important to me," Izenberg said. "When the kid dropped the bottle of milk and didn't want to tell his mother, you knew that he was a Polish-American because he would say all the mannerisms. That stuff is important."

On Red Smith (1905-92), whom he sat side-by-side with at the New York Herald Tribune sports desk early in his newspaper career: "We were quite friendly. He was very nice to me," Izenberg says now.

"People ask me about Red Smith because of my writing and my analogies and stuff, they say, well, you must have really been heavily influenced by Red."

He went on: "To me, the biggest thing Red Smith did for me, that he did for all sportswriters, was give them permission to write the English language. And that's it."

Now, decades after his first published articles, Izenberg admitted that "believe me, it took a long time to make my (writing style)."

Who had the biggest influence?

Jimmy Cannon (1909-73), whose career includes stops at the New York Daily News, New York Post, Newsday and New York Journal-American, plus Stars and Stripes as a World War II correspondent. (One memorable zinger from Cannon's collection: "If Howard Cosell were a sport, he'd be roller derby.")

Why?

"Because Jimmy Cannon taught me just by reading him—and of course I traveled with him and I knew him—his writing taught me everybody doesn't speak the same way," Izenberg said. "When he interviewed Joe Louis, he wouldn't change the grammar as other writers would do. He'd write it the way Louis said it. That became very important and he'd try to convey who this person was. You don't have the cheating luxury of television, you know, which is you show pictures and people get distracted by the pictures, and it really doesn't matter what the hell you say, because they are not readers anyway, they are voyeurs as people who are so heavily influenced by television as viewers. And (as print journalists you've got to try to paint as many pictures as you can.

"Cannon was the great voice. He was terrific, and that's because he did a lot of things, which I did—a lot of things.

"I must have done every job you can do on a newspaper, and you know, chasing fire engines and stuff like that is really more important than saying, look, I know all the statistics about Major League Baseball. That's why they have record books. You've got to be a reporter first to be a columnist. You have to be a reporter first, but you've also got to be an interpreter. Columnists give you perspective if they're any good. Today, there ain't many of them."

On Jim Murray (1919-98), whose tenure at the Los Angeles Times lasted from 1961-98 (and who once wrote of the Indianapolis 500, "Gentlemen, start your coffins."): "He was an extremely close friend of mine," Izenberg admitted. "We worked on opposite coasts and whenever we were going to the same place, we always hooked up with each other.

"Murray did not start out as a sportswriter. He was a movie critic for Time magazine ... and he brought a more expansive perspective, because I'm always looking for perspective when you write. I think you have to, because if you're a columnist—that's why it's so wonderful—and I once worked for an editor-in-chief who said, 'You wrote something about television the other day and I don't want to see it in the paper again because those people are trying to put us out of business (in the 1960s and '70s).' ...

"And I said, 'I love television. I go to the World Series and I don't have to tell anybody who won the game. They all saw it. Now I can tell them what they didn't see.' "

Perspective goes above and beyond the obvious facts. It connects the facts and delivers the details as narrative.

"Jim Murray was a perspective writer," Izenberg said. "If you want to know how great a writer Jim Murray was, I'll refer you to a column when he went temporarily blind for a while."

That column left a lasting impression on Izenberg and readers from around the country.

"About a week later—he was so respected The Times gave him somebody to accompany him and do the typing and whatever else till he got his sight back—he wrote a column about what he wants just once more chance to see: the sunset over the Pacific, that kind of stuff. And that's writing because you're suffering in your writing, but you're conveying. That's perspective."

Murray's column ("If You're Expecting One-Liners, Wait, a Column") gave readers a real look at his loss of vision and his never-wavering dedication to column writing.

With clear language and imagery, Murray wrote this in August 1998: *"OK, bang the drum slowly, professor. Muffle the cymbals and the laugh track. You might say that Old Blue Eye is back. But that's as funny as this is going to get.*

"I feel I owe my friends an explanation as to where I've been all these weeks. Believe me, I would rather have been in a press box. ...

"We read a lot of books together, we did a lot of crossword puzzles together, we saw films together. He had a pretty exciting life. He saw Babe Ruth hit a home run when we were both 12 years old. He saw Willie Mays steal second base, he saw Maury Wills steal his 104th base. He saw Rocky Marciano get up.

"I thought he led a pretty good life. ...

"You see, the friend I lost was my eye. My good eye. The other eye, the right one, we've been carrying for years. We just let him tag along like Don Quixote's nag. It's been a long time since he could read the number on a halfback or tell whether a ball was fair or foul or even which fighter was down.

"So, one blue eye missing and the other misses a lot.

"So my best friend left me, at least temporarily, in a twilight world where it's always 8 o'clock on a summer night."

Izenberg also holds great esteem for the late W.C. Heinz (1915-2008), the gifted columnist and magazine writer, whose 1958 book "The Professional" is "maybe the greatest boxing book ever written."

Chapter 2 : Influences and Memories

Jerry Izenberg has met and written about countless renowned figures, including Pele, Muhammad Ali and Nelson Mandela, over the years. And he's written about each of them with an authoritative voice and a recognition of each individual's standing in society and what they stand for.

For instance, Izenberg's meeting with Mandela at the 1992 Barcelona Olympics.

Here's how the column began:

"The old welterweight sat alone near the top rows of the balcony, a silver-haired man in a gray business suit ... without retinue ... without security people ... in truth, without anyone on either side of him.

"That would have been too distracting. In another incarnation, as a young man, Nelson Mandela was an amateur boxer ... that was before Robben Island, where they could not break him, and the other prisons that followed.

"They locked him up for 27 years, during which he remained the spark that kept the fire that burned for freedom in dozens of wretched South African townships, like Soweto, Alexandra and Langa. And when Mandela's time came, he built a nation that demanded that skin color become less and less important.

"Before his release from prison and his presidency, skin color had been everything wrong in South Africa. They called it apartheid. Now it was legally and, for most morally, dead primarily because of one man's journey.

"That was the road Mandela traveled to the Olympic boxing venue of the Pavelló Club Joventut de Badalona ... waiting that day through much of a three-hour card ... waiting to see just one fight. As he would tell me after it was over: 'What is important is not that we lost. What is important is that we are here, back where we belong in the way that we now belong.'

"It was a day I will never forget. I had left ringside to buy a soft drink and on the way back to my seat I happened to look up at the spectators' gallery.

"When I saw him, I thought I had to be mistaken. But I had seen too many photographs not to follow my hunch. I climbed the stairs to be sure and I walked over to him and I told him my name and the name of my newspaper and asked him for a few minutes. He smiled and gestured to the seat next to him and said:

" 'Not now. Our fighter is coming into the ring. Sit, sit we will talk later. You know I was once an amateur boxer.' "

The column illustrates how he developed as an important voice in sports media, and continues to be one of the leading experts and historians on a wide range of sports.

Izenberg's thirst for knowledge and commitment to storytelling never wavered.

Moreover, his ability to shed light on important societal issues off the court, or away from the stadium or arena gave him a platform to reach the masses via the printed word.

His column, appearing in The Star-Ledger since 1962, has received broader exposure over the decades through syndication.

In his so-called golden years, Izenberg still puts in the time and effort to give readers unique, fresh insights and important historical perspectives.

In a poignant essay, "Jerry Izenberg: An Appreciation" from his book "Thomas Hauser on Sports: Remembering the Journey," fellow boxing writer Thomas Hauser, Izenberg explained why sports are an important staple of American culture and daily life.

"Sports at its best is a great thing," Izenberg told Hauser. "It's who we are. All of us who were alive at the time remember where we were when John Kennedy was shot, when men landed on the moon, when the World Trade Center was attacked. But for a lot of Americans, the preponderance of common unifying memories revolve around sports."

***

Izenberg continued a discussion about influential journalists, including some he considered mentors, with a classic rant while simultaneously reflecting on some of the premier columnists of the 20th century.

"Those legacies, I was in the middle generation. I was in the generation after the giants," he said, referring to Red Smith, Jim Murray, Jimmy Cannon and Shirley Povich, among others. "People sometimes say to me you're one of them, but they don't know what they are talking about, and my generation was the ones who accepted their legacies. What followed us, forget about it. We don't have a legacy. Everything is on YouTube and if anybody writes anything at the end of something I write, it's Charlie from Cincinnati, or Big Joe from Hoboken, I don't answer anything. Fuck it. If they don't put their (full) name on it, the hell with them. I've got to put my name on it every day. Fuck them.

"But you'd be amazed with one phenomenon, which I've never discussed with my paper," he went on.

"When I write a piece that resonates, I can get as many as 80 emails directly to me. They will not write it at the end (of the article) on the website because we have a relationship."

Yet with humility, Izenberg stated that "I don't think I have a legacy that anybody cares about, but there are still people in their 50s who tell me I was their homework assignment all over Newark. Well, yeah, (at school) they would recommend that you read this thing (The Star-Ledger)..." He cited examples of students' required reading in sixth, seventh and eighth grades.

Izenberg underwent a double-spinal procedure several years back and goes to physical rehabilitation "because I want to walk, and I've got the same guy who was in Larry Holmes' corner before Larry Holmes tore his bicep and our relationship goes back 40 years. His place is unbelievable. I'm walking but I have pain, but I know how to deal with it."

He uses a wheelchair in airports because of the difficulty of walking long distances, but still flies for leisure and for work.

***

The question of legacy was a major thread in one interview that covered a few dozen topics.

Exhibit A: Shirley Povich (1905-98), who began working for The Washington Post in 1923 and filed stories until '98, left behind one of the biggest legacies.

Povich's remarkable longevity was only one part of his legacy, wrote Florida-based sports columnist Mike Bianchi after his death. "Maybe you've never heard of Shirley Povich or never read one of his sports columns—and that's too bad," Bianchi wrote.

"For the past 75 years, he waxed eloquently for The Washington Post, where he didn't just write sports, he changed sports. Where he didn't just make you laugh or make you cry, he made you think. Where his columns were home runs not so much because he hit them over the outfield fence, but because he saw beyond the outfield fence." And he became sports editor in 1925. Two years before that, he was attending Georgetown University as a law student.

"Povich was a legacy guy," Izenberg recalled.

What else?

"He was a fellow who spoke in measured language ... and he had tremendous respect for the language and tremendous respect for being ethical," Izenberg said. "And I'm going to tell you where he took it to the point where he took ethics.

"He went to Chicago to cover a world championship fight, which everybody did. Those heavyweight fights were dynamite. And he's talking to a cop who he knew for years. And the cop says, I know you like to hang out and go over there, and I'm going to say Big Sam, but I don't know what the guy's name was, but he was the guy who ran all the bookmakers in Chicago. He said, Don't go over there the day after tomorrow because we are going to bust the place.

"So Shirley felt honor-bound to tell Big Sam, who he'd always given the odds. Shirley never gambled but he gave him insight into events. So he calls him up and he says, Big Sam or whatever his name was, listen, they are going to bust your place in two days and I thought you should know. So when they busted it there were a bunch of old ladies sitting, knitting and talking to each other or they were a book club, and this and that There was no evidence of anything.

"Now he covers the fight, and the next morning he's going to fly home that night to Washington. The next day he comes down for breakfast and he always had milk toast for breakfast, and he sees Big Sam or whatever his name was, sitting there. (He says), Shirley sit at my table, and Shirley says, I would like separate checks.

"And he says, listen, Shirley, I owe you for what you did for me. I can't get over it. I got a tailor in this town, nobody has to know. Joe makes you two suits at my expense, and Shirley says, I can't accept it and I won't accept it. I did it because you're a nice guy and I did it out of friendship. ... You're not going to give me anything, you're not going to give me money.

"(Big Sam or whatever his name was) said, meet me in the coffee shop here in an hour and he runs out of the place. He comes back, he's got an envelope, he stuffs it into Shirley's inside pocket and takes off, and Shirley opens the envelope and it's the key to all of the pay toilets in Chicago ... and he laughed about it and couldn't wait to tell me the story."

Izenberg described Povich as "an astute writer, understood perspective, and had to compete with the guy who never got real good recognition outside of our business named Mo Siegel (1915-94, a sports columnist who wrote for The Washington Times, The Washington Star, The Washington Daily News and The Washington Post over the years), ... "and he was the funniest guy writing on the East Coast. And he was Shirley's competition and Shirley loved reading him and meeting him on the days when they spoke.

"But Shirley stuck to what Shirley did. Shirley was a straight-ahead writer. His command of the English (language) was excellent, but he measured his words. ... He didn't try to impress you, he tried to inform you."

***

Asked about Wendell Smith (1914-72), an African-American journalist who chronicled Jackie Robinson's career and the seminal moments of the 1947 season, when Robinson joined the Brooklyn Dodgers and broke Major League Baseball's color barrier, Izenberg said "he thinks of two people: Wendell Smith and Sam Lacy."

He went on: "They were the pioneers. Wendell Smith, unlike Sam Lacy, translated his ability as a great sportswriter, a great sports columnist really, he translated it into bridging the gap between the black and traditionally white press. ...

"Of course, historically, he was Boswell to Jackie Robinson, he traveled with him in Montreal (in the International League in 1946) and with the Dodgers, and he had a lot of courage."

Over the years, Smith wrote for the Pittsburgh Courier, an African-American newspaper, and later joined the Chicago Herald-American and Chicago Sun-Times in addition to working as a TV sports anchor for WGN in the Windy City. Smith was portrayed by actor André Holland in the 2013 film "42" about Robinson. Lacy wasn't portrayed in the film.

Smith was posthumously named the 2014 Red Smith Award winner, which is presented annually by The Associated Press Sports Editors. Lacy received the distinguished honor in 1998.

"They idolized him because he had the guts to write what the others didn't," Izenberg said of Lacy. "So many of those guys were on the take. They got to live; the paper wouldn't pay them anything, the black papers didn't pay anything. And this guy was unbelievable."

Izenberg believes that Lacy (1903-2003) was "overlooked over the years." Eventually, he became the first card-carrying black member of the Baseball Writers' Association of America and was inducted into the sportswriter's wing of the National Baseball Hall of Fame in Cooperstown, New York.

"And he was granted that right grudgingly so," Izenberg said of Lacy's BBWAA membership, "and Wendell went through the same things. It's just that I knew Sam better, and he told me more."

When Lacy passed away in 2003, Lacy had worked for the Baltimore Afro-American for almost 60 years.

For years, Lacy advocated the abolition of racial segregation in baseball. "The Negro Leagues were an institution, but they were the very thing we wanted to get rid of because they were a symbol of segregation," Lacy was quoted as saying in his New York Times obituary.

Izenberg remembered hearing about a Cincinnati Reds-Cleveland Indians exhibition game that was held in New Orleans, where Lacy took his BBWAA press card, "and the press box attendant sticks his arm across the entrance there and says, 'What are you doing here, nigger?' And he pulls out the card.

"(The attendant responded) by saying, 'Stick that card up your ass. No nigger's getting in my press box.'"

Lacy's response, according to Izenberg: "Well, there's only two black guys in baseball (Robinson and Larry Doby of Cleveland) and one of them's in this game and I'm going to cover this game."

"He said, 'You want to cover this game? Take a folding chair from over there and sit on the roof.'"

Lacy walked up to the roof, sat down and did his job: reporting on baseball.

"Nobody knows who he is or what he's doing. He's the only one up there," Izenberg said. "People are pointing and talking, and he's got his scorebook out and a bottle of water and he's got to cover the game.

"About the fifth or sixth inning, there's a commotion, and there was a metal ladder he had to climb to get to the roof, and here come these four New York writers up the ladder with folding chairs and they sit next to him.

"And he says, 'What are you fellas doing here? And the guys said we want to get a little sun; it's stifling in the press box.' Now when Sam tells me the story he said those white boys were in spring training for like a month. They were as dark as I am because I'm a light-skinned black man. They didn't need any sun. And that is one of the great stories."

Izenberg continued: "There were twice as many guys who didn't want him in that press box as those who did, or any press box. ... But these guys were better humans."

Many years later, another Lacy story also left an impression on Izenberg.

"Anyway, Sam wanted to give Muhammad Ali a plaque in Baltimore at the Baltimore mosque. Now Sam's wife was very, very light-skinned. ... So they are walking up the steps, it's an old synagogue or an old church that the Nation of Islam has taken over, bought, you know, and he's got the plaque under his arms. And the guy comes out (from the mosque) and says to Sam, Sam it's so good to see you, but that white lady can't come in here. Well Sam didn't say she's not white. Sam didn't say that she was black.

"He didn't say anything like that at all. He didn't say it was his wife. He said, Well, if she's not coming, I'm not coming, and the guy's standing there looking at them, and they are walking down these steps.

"He gets halfway, turns around, waves, puts the plaque on the steps, turns around and walks out. Now that's making a statement. That was Sam Lacy."

***

On Dick Schaap (1934-2001, journalist, author, TV and radio broadcaster, theater critic): "Dick Schaap was a terrific guy. I knew him when he was the sports editor of Newsweek and editor-in-chief (John) Denson had taken over the (New York) Herald Tribune. I had gone and quit, I was back in New Jersey," Izenberg said.

"And Dick became the city editor (in 1964) ... and it was not his milieu. He found his milieu. Dick Schaap was a brilliant television reporter. He would not be considered so by the arrested developments who watch a lot of these guys today because he didn't shout, he didn't curse, he didn't yell at anybody, he didn't make fun of anybody. He was a great reporter.

"When I knew him, (legendary NFL coach Vince) Lombardi was a friend of mine, and he portrayed Lombardi like he had never been portrayed before, which means as he was," he said, recalling Schaap's collaboration with Green Bay Packers offensive lineman Jerry Kramer in the best-selling 1968 book "Instant Replay" about the champions of the inaugural Super Bowl.

"It was a great dissection of the team that won the championship the hard way," Izenberg noted.

Schaap was a real people person who cultivated relationships with individuals from all walks of life, not just athletes.

"The right athletes gravitated toward him," Izenberg said of Schaap."They gravitated to (Howard) Cosell a lot of them, because Cosell would make them important. But the good ones gravitated toward Dick because they understood he was a cerebral writer and more than that a cerebral talker. And his legacy may last because of the milieu of television."

Chapter 3: More Influences

Since the Watergate scandal unfolded in the early 1970s, Bob Woodward's name has been a permanent fixture in journalism. His Washington Post articles, solo bylines or those written with his tag-team partner Carl Bernstein, guaranteed his importance for decades to come, even before the many books, movies and lecture circuit appearances.

Indeed, Woodward holds a prominent place in American society as a chronicler of the corrupt, monomaniacal Nixon presidency.

But decades earlier, another journalist with the same surname, Stanley Woodward (1895-1964), rose to prominence as a sports editor at the New York Herald Tribune, serving two stints as department boss (1933-48 and 1959-62). Some considered Woodward the best sports editor of all time.

With clarity and passion and wit and incredible details, Jerry Izenberg dished out keen insights on the huge impact that Woodward made on his life.

For starters, a key fact: inimitable columnist Red Smith and Izenberg both worked under Woodward.

In a 2006 column, Izenberg wrote about Woodward's integrity and moral convictions: "As sports editor of the Herald Tribune in 1947, he got wind that the St. Louis Cardinals had pledged not to take the field against the Dodgers if Jackie Robinson were allowed to play. Stanley, knowing such a strike could spread and derail the integration of baseball, called National League President Ford Frick.

"I am working on a front-page story about how the Cardinals are scheming to strike against Robinson tomorrow and about how you will decline to take action. It will run tomorrow—unless, of course, you get off your bureaucratic ass and stop this thing today, in which case I will tell everyone I meet what a fine fellow and hero you are.

"The Cardinals never struck. Frick got the credit as promised. All Stanley did was change history."

***

Izenberg learned a lot about the power of the press from Woodward. He learned how to do the job the right way, and he never forgot the lessons that his mentor taught him.

"I worked for the greatest sports editor and I think the greatest editor who ever lived. His name was Stanley Woodward," Izenberg declared. "I worked for him in Newark and I worked for him at the Herald Tribune. He went to Amherst College and he studied (a combined) seven years of Latin and Greek, in college. He would read 'The Odyssey' in Greek.

"This guy sent me on my first spring training (in 1959) and I'll never forget it. I went to Arizona and the Giants were there, and after three days he called me up on the phone. He'd say, 'Listen young man'—and when he said young man, then I knew I was in trouble. He'd say, 'Listen young man, I want you in my office in two days. I said, 'But I'm in Phoenix.' He said, 'You'll be finished if you're not in my office in two days.' I don't know what the hell I did, so I got there.

"And I walked in and he said, 'Who's going to play second base for the Giants?'

"I said, 'Well, that's an interesting question because there's seven guys at the same position.'

"And he said, 'I didn't ask you that; I asked you who's going to play it.'

"And I said, 'I don't know yet.'

"He said, 'I don't know anything about it at all. Let me tell you something (about your articles): Stop godding up athletes ... and don't be so full of yourself. I don't give a shit about the Painted Desert. I don't give a damn that the Lost Dutchman's Mine was only a mile and a half away from where (players) were returning. I want to know who the fuck is gonna play second base for the Giants. Now you sit down and you figure it out,' " Izenberg recalled his boss telling him.

Punishment followed.

The young man was in Woodward's doghouse.

"He took me off all writing assignments," Izenberg said of the great editor.

"And for two months I sat on that (copy) desk, and he didn't speak to me ... and I was dying."

Why's that?

"So it's like (quarterback Phil) Simms once told me, which was why (New York Giants coach Bill) Parcells was such a genius, when football coaches don't speak to you, you go crazy, trying to wonder whether you did something wrong or not," Izenberg related. "And it's the same about editors and writers who care about writing."

Izenberg's new routine after being ordered to return from Arizona was "desk, desk, desk" at the Herald Tribune.

Then, one day, "I looked at the schedule," he recalled, "and it was desk, desk, desk, Anderson Memorial Golf Tournament. I didn't know what the hell that was and I went to the slot man, the guy who ran (the sports desk) at night, and I said, what's this? He said, 'Jerry, it's nothing. It's a society golf tournament that the Tribune feels compelled to cover, and if you write more than a page it's going in the garbage.'

He continued: "So I go and I found out that the tournament is in Montauk (at the far end of Long Island, New York) and I'm living at that time in Maplewood, New Jersey. It's like going to the end of the world to get to Montauk. I got to get up at 5:30 in the morning to get up there for the tournament.

"I wander in and I'm the first one in the locker room and there's a guy shining shoes who says, 'Who are you? What are you in my locker room for?'

"I said, 'I'm covering the Anderson.'

"He said, 'Oh, they're going to cover that? You're kidding me.' "

About 10 minutes pass, Izenberg is sitting down and a man walks into the room and the small talk in the room, involving this golfer and the shoe-shine man, leads to Izenberg finding out "the man was in an automobile accident and he went through the windshield and he had glass in his eyes, and I think maybe it's been a month that he's been playing golf once a week.

"So I said to the guy, 'Do you mind if I walk around with you today?'

"He said, 'At this hour, I'll take anything for protection. ... It's you, the milkman and me apparently.'

"Well, he plays the round and he talks about everything while we're talking and what it means to see again. It's coming back."

That fueled Izenberg's desire to write an article to the length he decided, not a predetermined length.

"So I said, well, fuck them. I'm writing two pages," he said. "If they don't like it, fuck 'em. So I write the two pages, and in those days we still had candy stores on the corner, where they carried the paper and when you're 12 or 13 you stand outside the store and make up all these sexual stories which aren't true ... that was the role of the candy store. I always maintain by eliminating front stoops and candy stores, public housing in America destroyed the culture.

"But anyway, so I rush out to the corner store and I grab the Tribune and I'm reading it and everything is in there. So I'm off that day and the next day I go to work, and I look at the schedule and it says, Izenberg: college basketball, college basketball, college basketball."

Now Izenberg was out of Woodward's doghouse.

"So Stanley looks at me and says, 'How do you like your new assignment?' " Izenberg recalled.

"I said I love it, but there's one thing.

"He said, 'What thing?'

"I said, 'You don't say what, you just say college basketball.'

"He said, 'Let me tell you something: Number one, I hire people because they can do the job; if they can't do the job, I fire 'em. I look with askance at a game where grown men wear short pants and use a ball and they can't hit each other. So I question the virility of it. So I don't really care about college basketball, but you better care...' "

Izenberg insists that under the legendary editor's watchful eye he was pushed and challenged more than other writers.

"Well, he was always hardest on me, and I never knew why," he said of Woodward.

"When he was dying I went up to see him in Connecticut and I hate bird watching and deer watching and shit like that. I'm a city guy, but he loved it. So I'd sit out there for hours with him, and he'd say, that bird is a yellow blah-blah-blah, you know, but he was dying and he meant so much in my life.

"He had really taken over as a surrogate father. My father had died just before Stanley went back to the Tribune (in 1959), so I couldn't figure out why he was so hard on me."

Before Woodward passed away he presented a book to Izenberg and included a note in it, "To Jerry Izenberg, the logical successor to (W.O.) McGeehan, (Grantland) Rice and Smith," Izenberg recalled, "and I was stunned.

"And years later when I was inducted into the National (Sportscasters and) Sportswriters Association Hall of Fame down in North Carolina, I got a letter from Ellen, his daughter, who I'd never met. ...

"And she said, 'Jerry, I'm so sorry. I should've written this letter much sooner.'

"She said, 'I'm so thrilled your plaque's going on the same wall that Papa's on, but I should have told you this years ago. When he was dying I tried to take his mind off the pain, so I'd sit on the edge of the bed and we'd talk about the two things that he cared about: college football and journalism...'"

Woodward's daughter's letter continued: "And one day I said to him, 'Who is the best you ever had? Was it Red Smith, Joe Palmer or maybe Jesse Abramson?' And he said, I can't say for sure yet, but I think I could say soon, and there's no doubt in my mind that it will be Jerry Izenberg.' And she told me that in the letter and I was stunned, and I mentioned that in my induction speech."

How much influence did Woodward have on Izenberg's career?

"My education under him was incredible," Izenberg mentioned without hesitation.

"Whatever ethics or integrity I have in journalism came from him. Although I would never use the word journalism in front of him. When I applied for the job—I had been at a paper called the Paterson News (in New Jersey)—I had been at The Star-Ledger before that in college, and when I came back from the service (during the Korean War) I didn't want to go back. The world wasn't quite ready for me.

"I wounded up on a weekly paper where I was the photographer, the ad salesman, the sports editor and the editor and on Wednesday nights on a flat-bed press the publisher and I would print the paper, and then I would take it about 3 in the morning, because it always came out on Thursday, to the different drops. And for that I got the next day off and I was earning $62.50 a week.

"And I was desperate. I had one kid already. I got a job at the Paterson News, a low-echelon daily paper in New Jersey, and I wrote a note to Stanley because he had come back and taken over the paper, and he told me to come in but I have no job. But I saw your clips.

"I didn't know this, but Stanley used to read clips all the time. I think he scouted writers. He brought Red (Smith) in from Philadelphia that way (to the New York Herald Tribune in 1945). So he said to me, 'I don't have a job for you now but I'm going to start reading you,' and he did, because in a month he called me. And the last thing he said, 'I almost blew the job.'"

For Izenberg, that memory remains vivid decades later.

"He said, 'Why do you want to go into this business?'

"And I said, 'Well, I've always wanted to be a journalist.'

"He looked at me," Izenberg went on, "as though I was scraping some dogshit off the bottom of his shoe, and he said, 'You're in the wrong building, young man. We don't have any journalists here. You want to be a journalist, you go to The New York Times, you get a three-piece suit, you rent, steal or buy a Phi Beta Kappa key, and they will send you to Lucerne and Geneva, Switzerland, to cover financial conferences, and then you will be a journalist. In this building, we only have newspaper men.' "

Talk about a point that resonated.

"I never forgot it," Izenber said decades later. "I never thought of myself as anything else, even when I started writing books or directing and writing television shows. I've just always been a newspaper man and I'll die a newspaper man."

***

Knowing how to conduct interviews is a vital skill for any journalist.

Which is why Izenberg offered these insights: "Most people know something. It doesn't matter what it is they know something. Sometimes they don't know they know it, and in conversation it's your job to bring it out."

What else has he learned over the years about the art of interviewing?

"No, there aren't any bad interviewers other than if he walks away from you," Izenberg said. "Then it's a non-interview. There are bad interviewers.

"You've got to find that chord, that magical chord where you can share it. It's hard to find now because of the money the players make, because of the endorsements, because of all the crap, because they are afraid of you now because you are talking about drugs and they might be using 'em, or you might say they are using 'em. All that plays a part.

"I was very lucky, I was in the last era—I say was, I'm still writing but the era's dead—I was a part of the last era in which you could actually get close to guys who were making that much.

"(Muhammad) Ali was one of my five best friends in the world. (Joe) Frazier) and (George) Foreman were right up there. Same with baseball players, same with all of them. There was a common denominator. The good ones treated you as someone who they could read because you were there. They respected what you wrote or they didn't, and that determined how the interview went.

"That era's gone ... and besides everything is television now."

Have some TV interviewers elevated the craft?

"There are some very good interviewers on television, I'm talking about sports only," he said. "I'm not saying there aren't but the vast preponderance of them are not."

Chapter 4: Unforgettable Baseball Memories

While the New York Yankees were collecting World Series titles year after year, Jerry Izenberg was developing a lifelong passion for baseball following his beloved Newark Bears in his New Jersey hometown in the 1930s.

Decades later, Izenberg vividly recalls the sights and sounds and personalities that made the Newark Bears an institution and a great International League team in that era. Owned by the New York Yankees, the Bears featured a number of players who became stars for the Yankees. They played their home games at Ruppert Stadium, named for Yankees owner Colonel Jacob "Jake" Ruppert, a beer mogul, who also owned the Newark farm club.

"When you would hear the Bears, growing up there, on the radio station ... (they had) an announce named Earl Harper," Izenberg recalled decades later. "And a guy hit a home run, and he (Harper) would throw a box of Wheaties (cereal) down the street behind home plate for the guy. It was a community. It's wholly different than it is now. It was a great community. It was a community thing where if you hit a home run at the right time ... you got a free hat from Adam's Hats. They had a booster club that met on Wednesdays, but I was too young to go to any of that..."

Looking back at the Great Depression-era baseball in Newark, Izenberg talks of the days when the ushers didn't follow a by-the-book set of rules.

"It was an unwritten rule. If you were a kid, you got to sneak into the ballpark without paying somehow," he explained. "If you stayed in the bleachers, they left you alone, unless it was a big weekend game or a big night game. But if you got into the grandstand, they'd kick you out of the park.

"So I get into the grandstand one day, I think I was 8 or 9 years old, and there was a pitcher walking down toward the bullpen," he went on, "and I'm asking him for an autograph, I'm leaning over the side. And I probably had three of them already, but I'm asking for another one.

"And when you are 9 years old, or 10, to you they're ballplayers, they're not people; they're not people who didn't get laid last night, or (have) stomach distress, or whose kid is sick. That's what happens with human beings...

"So I was a snide kid. I had found a scorecard on the ground and he picked it up and threw it in the air and kept walking."

Izenberg would never forget it.

"Well, I was devastated," Izenberg, the longtime columnist says now. "I mean, if this had been the Toronto Maple Leafs or the Jersey City Giants, I could understand but this is bigger—one of my guys. And I'm fighting back tears and a woman comes and takes me by the arm and says, 'Come with me.'

"And I figure, 'Oh, god, she works for the ballclub, and I'm going to get kicked out.'

"And she walks me down the third-base line, which was where the Bears dugout was, and there's a group of women sitting and she says, 'Sit with these women. I'll be right back.'

"And so I'm sitting there and I don't know what the hell's happening, and she walks down the steps and leans into the Bears dugout. She comes back with the baseball. And she's got it in her hand and she puts it in my hand. And she says, 'This is an autographed baseball with every member of the team on it.'

"And I looked at her like she came from outer space."

Then the woman proceeded to ask Izenberg a question: "Have you ever heard of (George) Stirnweiss?"

His response?

"Oh yeah, I come to watch him all the time."

"Well, I'm Mrs. George Stirnweiss."

From 1943-50, Stirnweiss, a second baseman nicknamed "Snuffy," played for the New York Yankees. He was an American League batting champion (1945, batting .309), which was lowest recorded top average in either the AL or NL since Elmer Flick of the Cleveland Naps (now called the Indians) led the Junior Circuit with a .308 average in 1905.

But back to their time in Newark and despite their age difference, Izenberg, not yet a teenager, and the ballplayer's wife became friends.

"I was just enthralled. I'd see her in the ballpark and I'd wave, and she'd wave back," Izenberg revealed.

He found a loyal supporter in her, too.

Or as Izenberg put it: "She'd tell the ladies (via an introduction), 'This is Jerry, and he's a friend of mine.

So if he has any trouble with the ushers, you bring him over and let him sit with you.' So it was a good summer."

Fast forward to Sept. 16, 1958, when there was a train disaster in New Jersey that killed a reported 48 passengers, including Stirnweiss, who was en route to New York for work.

"So I wrote a column about it and about her," he said.

"About two weeks later, I got this neatly typed envelope. I opened it up ... and I cannot read one word, and there's a little typed note that says, 'I am Mrs. Stirnweiss's nurse, but she wanted to write this herself. If you can't understand this, she's really saying that she'll never forget you.

"That's a wonderful postscript but it's not the end of the story."

What happened next?

"Years later," he went on, "when I was writing this autobiography ("Through My Eyes: A Sports Writer's 58-Year Journey," published in 2009), I had some confusion about where she was from, or whether she was from Newark or whatever, and I knew that her husband had coached football at Red Bank Catholic High School at one time.

"I called down there and they had no records of anything, but the guy said, 'We know who he is and his daughter tended bar down here. So I called the bar and the guy said, 'She doesn't work here anymore, but she comes in a lot on weekends. I'll tell her you're looking for her,' because he knew who I was because of The Ledger.

"So about a week later the phone rings and it's a woman on the phone and she says, 'Is this Jerry Izenberg?'

"Yes."

And what was her response? "At last we meet. The little boy with the baseball. My mother told me that story a thousand times."

***

Without hesitation, Izenberg admits his childhood revolved around baseball—and understandably so.

"My father (Harry) had been a professional baseball player," he points out. "Long before I was born. If you put that together, you can understand baseball was my love for years and years and years. Not so much anymore, but then it was.

"That sort of was my boyhood, centered around the Bears and my father one day said to me—(and) he never had any money; during the Depression he worked seven days a week in a dye house—'What are you doing Saturday?'

"I might have been 11 or 12. I said, 'Playing ball.'

"He said, 'No you're not.'

"I said, 'I didn't do anything.'

"He said, 'Don't worry about it. You're going with me. I've got tickets somewheres.'

"So we get on the bus and we go to New York, and we get off the bus and we get on the subway. Now I had never been on a subway—and that's exciting for a kid, you know?

"And then we're underground, we come out and we started walking up the steps, and there it is in front of me, the Polo Grounds. There should have been organ music or something. I was going to the cathedral of Notre Dame, and it's all sold out.

"So my father says, 'Are you selling standing-room (only tickets) still?' And the guy says, 'Yeah, we're selling some standing room.'

"Well, I want two tickets," Izenberg remembered his father saying.

"And we went and we walked up the ramps that lead to the upper decks, and we stood on the ramp and all I could see was the pitcher's mound, and my father said, 'Don't worry, that's all you need to see.' "

Longtime Giants star Carl "Meal Ticket" Hubbell started the game for the Giants—"My father called him the greatest left-hander that ever was. That's his opinion, but I think it was pretty close to it."—in a contest against the Brooklyn Dodgers, "who had the most loyal following of any baseball team in America."

The Dodgers were the stronger team in those days, noted Izenberg. And even in the crosstown clashes, when the games were held in Upper Manhattan, crowds of 50,000-plus packed the Polo Grounds to watch the Dodgers and Giants, but "it was predominantly Brooklyn (supporters)."

In Izenberg's recollection, Hubbell tossed six innings that day, "six magnificent shutout innings, with my father saying, 'Watch this, look at that,' and then the Dodgers just kicked the crap out of 'em."

"He was at the end of his career and he pitched with his head," said Izenberg.

"So Mel Ott, who was the manager, comes out to get him and my father says, 'You should cheer because this might be the last time anyone sees him pitch,' and as he's leaving the field, the whole stadium, which was predominantly Dodgers, stands up and cheers for him, and it said a lot about the way baseball was followed and played in those days."

In summary, Izenberg described it all this way: "That was my baseball boyhood. I was not a very good player. I played second base because that's what my father played."

***

When it came to covering baseball, Izenberg said "he had the greatest rapport" with Roger Maris of the New York Yankees, the left-handed slugger who surpassed Babe Ruth's record of 60 home runs in 1927 with his remarkable 61 in 1961.

Through his work covering the Yankees, Izenberg would see Maris on a regular basis.

It involved an honest give-and-take. Or as Izenberg put it: "I'd come over and he'd say, 'I just don't feel like talking today,' and I'd say, 'Well, that's OK.' "

Maris was bombarded with questions like "Why didn't you hit a home run today?" Izenberg recalled.

"And then all these people (are ordered) to get the women's angle, get this, get that. People who don't know a baseball from an egg are asking these idiotic questions ... and the thing of it was Maris was very forthcoming with me, and I knew the Maris that other people didn't know."

Such as?

"People wanted to talk about how rotten he was," Izenberg said.

The columnist offered a much different point of view.

"(In 1985), Maris is dying of cancer in (Houston) in the hospital, and really dying—he's dead about 15 days later. ... And he's in tremendous pain, but he really is getting a rapport with his doctors," Izenberg said.

One of the doctors informed the ailing Maris about "a new experimental drug that they'd like permission to try it on you," Izenberg said.

Maris asked for details.

One of the doctors then said, according to Izenberg, "Roger, I've got to be honest with you. I don't know what it's going to do. But we've got to find out because it may be of importance to us, and it's not going to cure you but it might help somebody else down the line."

And how did the former baseball slugger react to the doctor's comments?

Maris said, "Go ahead. I'll take the drug."

Years later, Izenberg sees how some viewpoints are difficult to alter.

"He got a bum rap," Izenberg said, "that he was a lazy outfielder."

Izenberg illustrated his point with a tale from the 1962 World Series—Game 7, Giants vs. Yankees at Candlestick Park. The Yankees won the game, 1-0, to claim their 20th world title. In that deciding game, in the ninth inning, Willie Mays slugged a two-out double to the right-field corner, and Maris fielded the ball.

The veteran scribe picks up the account here: "Roger Maris threw a ball from the outfield that kept (Matty Alou) on third base (and prevented him from tying the game). If he doesn't make that throw, they could've lost the game.

"Then everyone forgets during the summer after his home run (record) ... that there'd be an announcement in the press box: The medical staff says about Roger's wrist it's a day-to-day proposition. They'd keep saying that.

"Well, it wasn't a fuckin' day-to-day proposition at all; it was never going to be the way it was. And, in fact, he played in the World Series and hit a home run and swung with one hand, one arm if you want to put it that way, because the wrist was so bad.

"But how did he break that wrist? And everyone in the press box would smirk when the PR guy said the day-to-day proposition.

"Well, shit, they were giving the impression that Roger was goofing off.

"How did Roger get that wrist (injury)?" he repeated. "Sliding home and an umpire stepped on it on a close play at the plate ... and they (the press) never bothered to explain that..."

What stands out about Izenberg's relationship with Maris?

"He was an interview that I was pleased that I could do what I needed to do," he revealed. "I didn't impose on him, but he didn't impose on me."

Chapter 5: How Music Shaped His Writing

Decades before his name was synonymous with Super Bowls, blockbuster prizefights, Triple Crown races and other marquee sports events, Jerry Izenberg was one of countless aspiring musicians in or near the Big Apple.

To this day, music influenced Izenberg's writing style.

"As a kid, I was a musician," Izenberg pointed out. "And that's what I intended to do for a living, and I played six instruments, I think."

A guy mentioned that he'd never heard about Izenberg's musical pursuits.

"Well, most people don't," he said, "because I don't like to talk about the things I didn't succeed at."

As a college student in northern New Jersey, not far from the bright lights and endless array of entertainment options in Gotham, Izenberg was captivated by the big city in the late 1940s and early '50s.

"I would go on weekends to New York and I would go down to 52nd Street—I was a jazz musician—and I would go to the Blue Angel and all the clubs on 52nd Street. They had a whole bunch of clubs, and sometimes I would go down to the Village to Eddie Condon's (club) or the Plaza, which was Dixieland," Izenberg recalled.

"I worked 40 hours a week at night when I went to college. But Saturdays, I didn't work, or Sundays. So Saturday, I would do that and I would get on a subway and go to Harlem at about 2 in the morning, and some of those places today I wouldn't go without a pet lion...

"I would sit in the clubs," he went on, "and the guys started to recognize me, the house bands, and one day a guy asked me to sit in. He said, 'Are you a musician?' and I said, 'Well, I'm not bad.'

"He said, 'What's the instrument that you like the most?'

"I said, 'I like the clarinet the most.'"

That led to one of the house band's members lending a clarinet to Izenberg, who took part in the group's performance.

The band didn't have sheet music to follow as it performed.

"I said that's OK," Izenberg remembered, "because everything's by ear with me, too. So I sat through that set and I froze on the solo, and they were very nice about everything. And they did me the biggest favor of my life because I walked out of there knowing if I try to do this for a living. I would make a living, (but) I would be teaching overprivileged kids in their home during the week and on weekends I'd be with some society orchestra that played weddings and bar mitzvahs and stuff like that.

"And I said that ain't for me."

Even though he didn't become a famous jazz musician, music became a valuable learning tool for the distinguished columnist.

Exhibit A: This column looks back on the 40th anniversary of The Thrilla in Manila, which showcases his lyrical approach to writing with musical rhythm as part of the overall structure: *"There are memories that cling to me with all the restraint of a second skin. Time doesn't blur their drama and the calendar doesn't lessen their impact,"* Izenberg wrote. *"So, I still see that day, 40 years ago in Manila on Oct. 1, 1975, as though it happened yesterday.*

"Muhammad Ali untouched by the physical and mental ravages of Parkinson's disease, an Ali who could still float like a butterfly and sting like a bee. Joe Frazier, ever narrowing the circle of combat, walking straight ahead into the line of fire with a head fake here, a shoulder dip there and a Philadelphia left hook that seemed to have a life and a will all its own.

"Together, they hammered out a message tinged with their personal histories and driven by their personal pride. The translation surely went like this:

"'Here we are again, caught in a web from which there is no escape, no love gained but no respect lost, and neither one of us will back ever back off.'

"In my tunnel of memory, I can still feel the oppressive heat in an arena without air-conditioning, still hear the roar of the crowd and still replay every memory of the drama between the 14th round that was and the 15th round that never happened.

"I learned an irrevocable truth that day. What I saw was not a battle for the heavyweight championship of the world. Each man knew a private truth in his heart. They were fighting for the championship of each other..."

Indeed, a powerful, scene-setting intro.

"I believe in the meter of words," Izenberg confessed on the telephone. "And ... there's a relationship between words and music and rhythm and that's the way I write.

"The best way to explain it is I use an example: The rumble of the subway train. The rattle of the taxis. The daffy-dills who entertain at Angelo's and Maxie's. That ('Lullaby of Broadway') was a great popular song in the '30s and '40s. And that's rhythm, that's music, as well as it is words."

Over the years, Izenberg's biggest gripe with his editors was in rewritten copy. He summed up "his biggest fights with editors" this way: "No, you cannot change that word. You are breaking up the rhythm of the sentence."

He added: "Also, you know, the crack of the bat on a home run is music. It's very different than a line-drive single."

One of Izenberg's trademarks in his columns is the use of an ellipsis, which has drawn criticism from some readers, including English professors. "But a lot of people love it," he pointed out.

Why does he use ellipses so frequently?

"Because a period means the end of the sentence," he said. "But an ellipsis means, wait a minute, stop and think. This is so connected I can't use a period to separate 'em. That goes back to my music. The ellipsis is a pause. It's like a rest on a sheet of music."

Chapter 6: Secretariat, American Pharoah and Canonero II

Secretariat's jaw-dropping, 31-length victory in the 105th running of the Belmont Stakes in June 1973 clinched the amazing horse's Triple Crown feat. It secured his place in the annals of the sport until the end of time.

And it was a performance that nobody thinks will ever be replicated.

Jerry Izenberg witnessed Secretariat's unparalleled greatness that day long ago in New York.

He also witnessed countless disappointments after Affirmed's Triple Crown quest in '78 until America Pharoah's thrilling triumph in the 2015 Belmont, which completed the rare feat.

Before and after the 42-year gap between Secretariat and American Pharoah's epic storylines, Izenberg chronicled the sport's modern-day history. Year after year, he covered the big races and remembered with great detail what transpired on the track.

"Go back to Secretariat, that was a thrill, and I can narrate that race for you right now where it starts," he said.

"He's got a life-and-death rivalry with Sham," he went on, referring to the horse that defeated him earlier that year in the Wood Memorial Stakes (Sham placed second; Secretariat took third).

"What never was public until many years later was that the reason Sham beat him was he had a defective wisdom tooth or molar, I guess, and when you pull the bit, what happens? Because the jockey didn't know and the owner didn't know. The trainer kept it a secret. So he lost that race. That was the great secret. ...

"Well, in the Derby, he kicks Sham's ass, and it continued, and when it came the day of the Belmont, (the trainer) said to his jockey, 'You take Sham. Wherever he goes, you go, like glue.'

"And it was the last race Sham ever ran because Secretariat broke him with the pace," Izenberg said.

An unprecedented pace, which forced TV broadcasting technical innovations.

Let Izenberg's words paint the picture and deliver the explanation:

"And the pace got so wild, that it was the first time television had to split the screen (for horse racing). They couldn't get the whole field in the picture, and Lucien Laurin, the trainer, said to Penny Tweedy (Chenery), the owner, 'Get me a gun. Get me a gun. I want to kill Ronnie (Ronnie Turcotte, the jockey). He's killing the horse. The horse is gonna break down.' And I said the same thing to the guy next to me, the late Bob Harding, God rest his soul, and he disagreed.

"He wanted to run."

And so he ran.

"And when they came down the stretch, Turcotte heard nothing," Izenberg said. "It's unusual. And having heard the roar of the crowd, he was looking for that horse (behind) him, but he didn't see anybody, so he turned in his saddle, which you can never do, and ... way back in Japan somewhere there's the rest of the horses."

In a conversation, Turcotte once told Izenberg about the closing seconds of that remarkable 1½-mile race.

"He turned and he looked at the heavens," Izenberg recalled Turcotte saying, "and he said, 'God ... if you love me, don't let me fall off this horse now.' "

"That was the greatest ride by a horse," Izenberg declared before relating another gem that Turcotte told him: "I wasn't the jockey. I was the passenger."

Indeed.

Secretariat's greatest performance was so much better than his foes that he remains the quintessential champion.

"Now I measure all horses against that and they all finish second or way off the track," Izenberg said before American Pharoah confirmed his greatness in the storybook final race of his career.

Recapping that Breeders' Cup Classic in Lexington, Kentucky, Izenberg wrote:

"There was nothing this horse didn't do—not during the Triple Crown races, not in the paddock on Saturday, not in the post parade, and most importantly when for the first time he was tested against older horses, which is the gold standard measurement for any Triple Crown winner."

As expressed in that column, it left no doubt in his mind that the 2015 Triple Crown winner had achieved greatness.

Throughout May and June 2015, when American Pharaoh etched his name in the annals of history, The Star-Ledger published a useful reminder of Izenberg's connection to the sport's history. The statement: *"Izenberg covered all nine races that produced the only Triple Crown winners since 1948—Secretariat, Seattle Slew and Affirmed."*

***

That said, the veteran columnist had a rooting interest in seeing the Bob Baffert-trained horse erase the 37-year Triple Crown drought.

Or as he put it: "I kind of hoped he did it because I'd seen so many failures."

He then talked about what he called "the most courageous failure that I ever saw."

"There was a horse brought in Kentucky that had a crooked leg ... and nobody was going to buy him. He's finally bought and resold to a guy from Venezuela, whose company I think makes toilet seats, and they rode him a couple times.

"Now he comes up and he's got the first black trainer in racing since early post-slavery days named Juan Arias. The horse can't win. Can't win. So after racing two or three races, they take him back home to Venezuela.

"And down in Venezuela, they have mile-and-a-half races, which we don't have normally."

The perpetual losing angered the owner, who blurted out these instructions, according to Izenberg: "He says, 'Listen, find a race at a mile-and-a-quarter that he can win to let him know what it's like to win a mile-and-a-quarter race.'

"Arias tells him, 'Well the Kentucky Derby's a mile-and-a-quarter...' "

That idea set the wheels in motion for jockey Gustavo Avila's improbable quest along with Canonero II in 1971.

"He starts to fly to Miami, halfway there there's engine trouble," Izenberg recalled. "You have to turn around and go back. They keep him on the runway while they are fixing the engine. He never gets out of the plane. He flies back to Miami and goes into quarantine. He's in quarantine for a week, 10 days, or whatever it is. He's losing weight. He looks terrible. But he's nominated (to enter the Derby), and in those days there's no limit on the field.

"And so Arias says to the owner, 'Listen, I can get him on a flight.' And he says, 'Fuck the flight business. It cost me enough money now. Put him out on a truck. Go out there on a truck.' And they do that.

"He gets there and he's (drawn) last in the Kentucky Derby. I think there were 21 horses that year (actually 20). Dead last, has to go outside all the way. Could have run to Cincinnati with the ground he covered, wins the damned race."

Then what?

"The hottest party ticket in Louisville is the trainer's party ... and no trainers show up. They had a black trainer. The Latin jockeys run through the back stretch and they've got all these Latin jockeys and they make a party.

"So he says to me before the second race, 'What are they saying about me?' Because they were talking about him all the time."

Izenberg changed the subject, saying it doesn't make a difference "because you can't win the Preakness. It's impossible. You've got to make a move early and then..."

"He says, 'OK, you watch, we'll go wire-to-wire.'

"And they did; they won it wire-to-wire."

Next stop: New York.

"And they don't want him to win the Triple Crown," Izenberg noted. "You talk about prejudice. They don't want it. Black guy, Latin jockey, Latin owner, and the New York Racing Association in its great traditional style blows the whole fuckin' thing.

"They're snobs. So the ads in the papers are: 'Test of champions, a mile-and-a-half. See who can do it.' The ads should've been in Spanish.

"So I'm standing on the roof before the Belmont ... and he's walking around, but he goes past the clubhouse side. They've all got their body language, dead silence, arms crossed..."

Canonero II is then seen by a large throng of New York's Latino community, whose spirited support included "people screaming, waving flags. There were Puerto Ricans that were waving Venezuelan flags," Izenberg recounted. "And that's the way it was."

Canonero II placed fourth in the Belmont Stakes, "and then we found out why he lost the race," Izenberg says now. The reason?

A nuisance known as thrush, a bacterial infection on the hoof that could be described as "the equine equivalent of athlete's foot."

It could not have been diagnosed at a worse time.

"They tried to pull him out of the race before the race, and the track (officials) knew what was wrong and they said, let him run, we'll talk to the veterinarians," Izenberg said. "People came here, we'll have the biggest crowd. It was a record crowd (82,694)."

"Well, some guy who I won't name, jumps up in the press box and says, 'I told you that black son of a bitch couldn't train.'

"That's why Canonero became one of my favorites," Izenberg concluded.

Chapter 7: On Courage and Heroism

Through the ages, scholars and sidewalk merchants, cashiers and chiropractors have contemplated what courage means as it applies to their daily lives. Different definitions are, of course, recognized by different groups during different eras in different societies.

Ernest Hemingway took a stab at defining its meaning and its importance.

"Few men are willing to brave the disapproval of their fellows, the censure of their colleagues, the wrath of their society," Hemingway wrote in "A Farewell to Arms."

"Moral courage is a rarer commodity than bravery in battle or great intelligence. Yet it is the one essential, vital quality of those who seek to change a world which yields most painfully to change."

In his long career as a sports columnist, Jerry Izenberg has seen more than a few athletes who can be considered courageous and brave.

Greco-Roman wrestler Jeff Blatnick occupies a special spot in this category.

More than 30 years after Blatnick's gold medal-winning triumph as a super heavyweight at the 1984 Los Angeles Summer Olympics, Izenberg remembered the challenges he had to endure to compete in California on the global stage, but first and foremost, to survive before even getting there.

"He develops cancer," Izenberg said. "He might die. He's living in upstate New York and he says to his parents, 'You can give me one great gift. Let me move out and move into the Y (YMCA). I'm gonna train. I'm gonna get better. I'm gonna take my radiation and whatever and I'll come home every weekend to spend with you, I promise.' "

Izenberg spoke about Blatnick's battle with Hodgkin's disease, which he was diagnosed with in 1982.

"But," he continued, relaying Blatnick's message to his parents, "no questions about, 'you don't look good, you didn't eat enough.'

"They go along with it. He comes back and he makes the Olympic team.

"Now somebody told me what a great story this is. So I got his name, and it's the (early days) of computers, and now I know why AT&T computers went out of business. ... I type his name under 'USA,' and it has his last name, first name and (information not found). Well they didn't know he was on the team; I found him because he won the gold medal, and I was there (in Anaheim), when he won it."

The Hartford Courant recounted Blatnick's Olympic triumph in a November 1996 article. "Cancer was a part of my life, a part of my life I had to deal with," Blatnick said, according to the article.

"But I learned that I could overcome adversity. Faith and attitude go hand in hand."

Looking back at Blatnick's gold-medal match, the Courant's Tommy Hine reported: "When the bout ended, Blatnick dropped to his knees, kissed the mat and crossed himself. Unable to maintain his composure through much of a television interview, he walked off camera, saw his parents and broke down and wept in his mother's arms."

To this day, Izenberg recognizes the meaning of Blatnick's accomplishment.

"It was a great story," Izenberg said.

"And a year and a half later, the cancer came back, and he said, 'Damn it, I'm gonna beat it again.' And he took radiation and at the last treatment (on Valentine's Day, in 1986) he shows up in a raincoat, and he opens the rain coat and he's got on tails. He flips this thing he's carrying and it's a top hat, and he's got a bottle of champagne for the nurses."

Pause for a moment to imagine that scene straight out of a made-for-TV movie.

Then listen to Izenberg continue his recollections of a conversation from the mid-1980s: "And I said, 'Why did you do that? Gratitude?'

"And he said, 'No, when is the last time anybody working in that (hospital) ward could smile? That's what I wanted and that's what I got.' "

Blatnick, who carried the U.S. flag at the Closing Ceremony during the '84 Summer Games, didn't compete at the 1988 Seoul Olympics. He became a wrestling coach at a high school in New York and devoted time to charitable causes and other endeavors. He joined the board of directors for Gilda's Club, the late comedienne Gilda Radner's support centers for those with cancer. (Blatnick established a Gilda's Club in New York.)

"Those are acts of heroism," Izenberg said.

Blatnick passed away at age 55 in October 2012. The cause of death was complications following heart surgery, media outlets reported.

***

Similarly, former MLB outfielder Jim Eisenreich, whose big-league career started in 1982 and wrapped up in '98, impressed Izenberg with his public fight against Tourette's Syndrome.

"When he was a little kid, other kids were not allowed to play with him," Izenberg pointed out.

And they'd call him every name in the book.

"You bastard, you son of a bitch," he said.

Then things got much worse before they got better, with his pro career on hold as a result.

MLB.com summed it up this way in a 2012 feature: "Eisenreich was on the voluntary retirement list between 1984 and 1987 while undergoing treatment for Tourette's, an illness which causes involuntary tics and vocal sounds. After getting the help he needed, Eisenreich signed with the Royals and jump-started a career which would last 13 more seasons."

But he had his awkward moments after leaving K.C., too.

"He decides when he gets traded to the Phillies (in 1993) he's not gonna speak," Izenberg recalled.

One day, he meets his teammates at training camp and during various interactions just nods his head and mutters "mmm, mmm, mmm," Izenberg said, recalling the details.

"Finally, somebody tells someone and they figure out what's going on. So just before the practice ends that day, a couple of them come over and they say, 'Well, Jim, nice talking with you.'

"And that becomes their slogan: nice talking with you."

That fall, Eisenreich hit a three-run home run in the Phillies' Game 2 win of the World Series over the Toronto Blue Jays at SkyDome. And he became an instantly recognizable positive role model for those affected with Tourette's Syndrome.

"That's courage," Izenberg said.

Indeed, Eisenreich blossomed into a role model and found his comfort zone as an athlete and teammate, learned how to cope with Tourette's. And as his playing career was winding down, Eisenreich established the Jim Eisenreich Foundation for Children with Tourette's Syndrome, which is based in Missouri.

"When I first talk to parents and their kids, they see me as a ballplayer," Eisenreich told MLB.com. "But then they begin to see me as a person."

Eisenreich also won a World Series with the Florida Marlins in '97.

Clearly, Izenberg understands the value of not focusing solely on those with wins next to their name.

Different character traits are revealed after losses. And those things can enrich a reporter's story or a columnist's copy.

"By choice, I went to an awful lot of losers' locker rooms," Izenberg said.

Chapter 8: Recollections of Fidel Castro and Other Cuban Tales

The geopolitical landscape—and realities—of the Cold War changed the world at a rapid pace.

Jerry Izenberg remembers those days and key individuals from that time.

In an interview, Izenberg talked about some of the great Cuban athletes, including dynamic Olympic champions in heavyweight boxer Teofilo Stevenson and middle-distance runner Alberto Juantorena, who excelled during the early years of the Castro regime.

Decades before he interviewed Nelson Mandela during an Olympic boxing tournament, Izenberg was interested in asking Fidel Castro one question.

Some background precedes that tale from a conference years ago...

"Every year of the Olympics, like six weeks before, they have the International Scientific Congress (promoted as 'Olympic Sport and Sport for All'), and they discuss all subjects of sports and I wa speaking about the frauds that take place during the Olympics," Izenberg said. "And also speaking with his own little group (at that event) was (Alberto) Juantorena, and we got to be friendly, and he told me Stevenson was his friend.

"And I said, 'I know Stevenson because he won the Olympics four times in 16 years. ... I said I want to go to Cuba, but they'll take my passport if I do, and I don't want that to happen,' " Izenberg recalled telling Juantorena.

"And he said, 'You can get on Mexican Airlines and go, and I can help you out with that. And why do you want to go?'

Juantorena handed Izenberg a business card "that he threw out recently." Printed on the card was the name of the chargé d'affaires at the United Nations "who we were dealing with occasionally from Cuba."

According to Juantorena, Izenberg remembered the great runner saying that the diplomatic contact "knows you very well. He said that if you show him this, maybe he can set you up with Castro. And then he said, 'Why do you want to do this? What is the one question you want to ask him?' "

"I said, 'I wanna see if I can get half an hour with Castro. I have one question I want to ask him about the boxing team and the way they train for the Olympics and how a little country wins so many golds."

Helping connect the dots from national leaders to the Olympics to interviews to boxing to baseball, Izenberg then mentioned Preston Gomez, who passed away in 2009. Born in Cuba, Gomez had a long career as a baseball manager, both in the minor leagues (Reds, Dodgers and Yankees farm systems) and in the bigs (Padres, Astros and Cubs).

Gomez, who played for the Washington Senators in 1944, also led the Havana Sugar Kings to the International League title in 1959 as their manager, and piloted the club to the Junior World Series crown the same year.

"His brother was arrested and sent to the Isle of Pines after the revolution," Izenberg said. "And he got his brother out because he knew Castro."

As the manager of the Sugar Kings (Cincinnati Reds affiliate), Gomez worked under owner Roberto "Bobby" Maduro, who lived in Miami at the time.

One day, Gomez told Izenberg a story about how shortly after the Cuban revolution the Sugar Kings played against an opponent and Castro, a former University of Havana pitcher, insisted that he wanted to pitch.

"So he stopped the game and came out of the stands and he wanted to pitch to one batter," Izenberg recounted, saying this unusual stoppage of play happened in 1960. "Well, he could do whatever the hell he wanted."

"Well, Castro threw three pitches that were like nine miles over the batter's head. It was strike one, strike two, strike three, and he cheered and they fired guns in the air and he went back in the crowd.

"Well, one of those balls landed near Gomez in the coaching box, and he called up Maduro and said, 'Listen, we're going on a road trip tomorrow and you're coming back after that without me. I ain't gonna stay here.'

"And Maduro said, 'Maybe we shouldn't stay, either.' "

"And that's how they made the arrangements to go to Jersey City, where they played half the season."

After the Castro regime nationalized all American-owned businesses that year, the Sugar Kings relocated to Jersey City, New Jersey, and became known as the Jersey City Jerseys.

Fast forward to November 2015, and the Castro regime was still in charge. And baseball has gone through massive changes in that span, though.

"There were so many interesting things happening in baseball in those days," Izenberg mentioned.

Chapter 9: Gratitude for Readers

An Izenberg column from November 2015 provided a revealing look at the tie that binds a trio of New Jersey coaching legends: Vince Lombardi, Mickey Corcoran and Bill Parcells.

Corcoran was mentored by Lombardi, an NFL legend, and played an instrumental role in shaping the coaching mind of Parcells, who became an NFL legend, too.

Izenberg traced the historical roots between the three men at St. Cecilia's Catholic School in Englewood, New Jersey, explaining how it all started with Lombardi, continued with Corcoran and followed with Parcells. It began with basketball at St. Cecilia's, where Lombardi, who received a pay raise of a couple hundred bucks by Father Tim Moore to add hoops to his busy workload, which already included football and physics, chemistry, and Latin.

So Lombardi "went to the public library and checked out a how-to basketball book written by Dana Bible, the old Texas A&M basketball coach. It was his play book," Izenberg wrote. "The rest was all due to Lombardi's intensity.

"And Corcoran, his star pupil, made it work. Together, they won a state title."

Fascinating stuff.

Izenberg sees the big picture and his historical perspective as a newspaper columnist and keen observer of American and global sports spans decades.

Furthermore, he also recognizes the role he's had—the enjoyment and thought-provoking material he's given to readers - for decades, too.

A gifted communicator, he's appeared as a frequent guest on two Irish sports radio programs for about two decades.

"We have a lot of fun because these people do their homework," Izenberg said. "They know how to interview and they are not starstruck by television. We do fine..."

When he decided to retire from his full-time columnist workload at The Star-Ledger at age 77, he signed a contract that kept him busy—penning about 50 columns a year. He became Columnist Emeritus.

"But I'm still writing, I'm still traveling, I'm still working," he pointed out.

Back to one of the Irish radio shows...

"This guy's interviewing me," Izenberg said. "He's doing a great job. He finishes up and comes to the very end and he says, '...I want to ask a question and I hope I don't embarrass you: Tell me, you know, for all these plaques and trophies and awards and all these things, the sportswriters (National Sportscasters and Sportswriters Association; the North Carolina-based organization has since changed its name to National Sports Media Association) Hall of Fame and this and that, whatever, the Red Smith Award ... Why didn't you ever win the Pulitzer?' "

His reply?

"I can't tell you why, but I can tell you what your question means to me," Izenberg recalled saying.

"I've been nominated 15 times and I'll tell you I'm not gonna say it's political ... I'm not even going to get into that. But I'm going to tell you this: At the height of my paper's circulation, we were a million and a half on Sunday and 650,000 daily. Now let's take a daily paper. Let's round it off to 600,000. If one out of every six readers reads my column every day, and I do believe they do, that means I have an extended family of at least 100,000.

"Now when I go to hang it up, if I can look in the mirror and say, 'Well, I tried, I gave it the best shot I had,' and if those hundred thousand can say, 'He did and he really gave us what we wanted, and sometimes what we needed,' ... if that can happen, what greater prize is there?

"I don't need the fuckin' Pulitzer."

***

Every year, Izenberg pens a Memorial Day column in honor of his father, Harry, who was a wounded American soldier in World War I.

"Anyway, this year when I went to write it, it was early. It's the same column; I just make little changes here and there," he said in 2015. "It was the day before Memorial Day and I get a phone call from this guy. He said, 'I'm the president of the Jewish War Veterans of New Jersey and I'm first calling for donations.' And I started to tell him, 'Listen, I gave at the office during the Korean War, so that's enough.' But that's not what happened.

"He said to me: 'Is there a flag on your father's grave?' "

Izenberg admitted he didn't know.

"He said, 'Well there ought to be.' "

"The next day, I get an email with three pictures. This guy got up at 6 in the morning, went to the cemetery—I told him where my mother and father were buried—and planted this flag on my father's grave. And in his email to me he said, 'Don't thank me. It's the least I could do for what he did, it's the least I could do for your service, and the least I could do for the pleasure you've given me all these years.

"That's a pretty good extended family," Izenberg said before admitting, "Well I cried when I saw the pictures."

Chapter 10: Friendship with Muhammad Ali

Jerry Izenberg has said Muhammad Ali "was one of my five best friends in the world."

But time marches on. Everything changes.

Ali, who passed away at age 74 in June 2016, and Izenberg weren't in close contact in recent years.

For Ali, the complications of Parkinson's disease and aging made it much harder for meaningful interaction on a regular basis.

"The last time I spoke to Ali was about four years ago, when we could still communicate," Izenberg said in 2015.

"But I'll tell you, we had a great relationship," he added.

What defined their relationship?

"I think the fact that No. 1 he understood that I understood more about Islam than most writers," Izenberg pointed out. "And also about the Nation of Islam, which is not Islam in my opinion, it's more an occult.

"And I saw the metamorphosis in Ali. I remember the time he came to make a speech for my particular charity, which I founded, and went crazy because he misplaced a prayer rug.

"This is a guy who, until he lost his marbles, was, and in his mind maybe still is, a devout Sunni Muslim. And I saw the transition from one thing to the other."

Izenberg noted that the legendary boxer liked "familiar things and my face was always there. ... That's when we began to make this rapport."

How so?

"We could joke with each other about religion even," added Izenberg. "I had a great respect for what he did and I never deified him."

On a PBS documentary, "The Trials of Muhammad Ali," released in 2014, Izenberg was asked to give his perspective on the former heavyweight champion.

"And I stand by the last thing I said, which they used to close the show: 'He wasn't a devil. He wasn't a saint. He just was Muhammad Ali, which was better than most people,' " Izenberg said.

Their friendship was easygoing and buoyed by talk—about practically anything.

"He would ask my opinion about things that he was really interested in," Izenberg recalled.

"And we covered so many wives, so many countries. Gene Kilroy, who was the business manager in his camp, who was much closer than that—he was a friend—and Gene is white ... and Gene and I were the two faces that were there all the time. All the time. And Jerry Lisker, who was the sports editor of the New York Post, God rest his soul, went with me to Ali's camp, I'll never forget it, just two weeks before Ali went to Africa for the Zaire fight (1974's The Rumble in the Jungle against George Foreman)."

There, in Deer Lake, Pennsylvania, Izenberg and Lisker walked in on a training session.

"Ali's hitting the heavy bag and I said to Jerry, 'What the hell's going on?' Ali had arthritis in both hands, which people did not know," Izenberg said. "He had not been able to hit the heavy bag for a year and a half, and he looks over his shoulder and sees us ... and he's banging the bag and he's saying, 'I'm gonna knock that sucker out. I'm gonna knock that sucker out. I'm gonna knock that sucker out.'

"And I say, 'You know something, Jerry? He's gonna do it.'

"I found out later how they healed his hand, and again I found that out from the guy who set it up and nobody else ever wrote it or knew it, and I don't even know if they knew he had bad hands because with (Dr. Ferdie) Pacheco always giving him shots and Novocain, crap, and they were saying that this doctor took him off all that and did something else.

"Anyway, I picked him to win by knockout. There were probably 35-40 guys there, two of us picked him by knockout, and it was Jerry Lisker and me."

Izenberg, of course, will never forget that.

Once while telling this story to another writer, Izenberg said, "Listen, just remember one thing: I remember the day he said to me a long, long time ago, 'If I say a mosquito can pull a plow, don't argue Hitch him up.' And that's why I picked him."

Before the turn of the century, ESPN selected Michael Jordan as the greatest athlete of the 1900s. Babe Ruth was selected at No. 2 and Ali was the No. 3 pick.

Izenberg disagreed with Jordan being selected No. 1.

"He only impacted on the shoe industry," Izenberg said of Jordan, "and kids who are idolizing the fact that they are going to get the kind of shoes that he had. A great player? One of the greatest who ever lived. But the impact on the era was Ali.

"Nobody was neutral on Muhammad Ali. That's impact. And that's how I felt about him."

***

Fifty-five years after Ali (then known as Cassius Clay) won a gold medal at the 1960 Rome Olympics, their friendship produced a tale for the ages.

Izenberg dished out the details with a movie director's eye for memorable scenes.

"I'll tell you how close we were," Izenberg said. "When he lit the torch for the (1996 Atlanta) Olympics, I called and he had a secretary called Kim out in Berrien Springs, Michigan. He bought (Al) Capone's old farm. I called her up that morning and I said, 'My paper's bothering me. Is he going to light the torch? I don't really care. But they want to know. I wanted to know for one reason: Whoever lit it was going to light it at night, and if it was him ... how could this man be chosen?' Nothing else was gonna change, and I could make more papers, because you're always fighting a deadline.'

"She said, 'Jerry, I don't even know if he's going to be there,'" Izenberg recalled.

"He's had an asthma attack."

Talk about a fly in the ointment for a columnist on deadline.

"She's lying to me. OK," Izenberg said, "because of a non-disclosure thing."

Fast forward to the Opening Ceremony.

"So I look up and I see him and he's doing it," Izenberg said, "and I'm so fuckin' mad, because now I've got to work. I could've had an easy night, right?

"So the next morning I get a phone call—this is how our relationship is—(and) I'm staying at the Holiday Inn, which is about 15 miles outside of town. I get a phone call and this voice says, 'Fooled you, didn't I?'

"And I said, 'Who is this?' I know who it was, of course.

"Muhammad."

"And I said, 'Muhammad Who?'

"He said, 'Muhammad Ali, the greatest of all time.'

"I said, 'The Muhammad Ali who told me he never tells a lie because he can't go to paradise if he does. That Muhammad Ali?'

"What are you talking about?"

"Well, Kim said you were in the hospital," Izenberg replied.

"He said, 'Well, Kim ain't no Muslim. She can lie.'

"And then he says, 'Come over here.'

"Where are you?"

Ali informed his friend he didn't know where he was. So his wife, Lonnie, got on the phone. She told Izenberg to stop by the Omni Hotel.

"We were registered under such-and-such a name," Izenberg recalled Lonnie Ali saying. "Come up, knock on the door and we'll let you in."

He arrives at the hotel.

A while later, the two old friends were alone. Ali lies down on the bed to rest and they begin talking.

"Now you can still understand him but you've got to a) know who he is; and b) if you know him, get accustomed to his voice. It always takes you a while to readjust. And he's going to say about five words, and you are going to have to translate that into a full paragraph," Izenberg said.

"And he's talking to me and he's talking about the closet, and I think he's saying someone's in the closet. I didn't know what the hell he sees, and he's mumbling, so I go and open it up. In the closet is the Olympic torch.

"I bring it back and I hand it to him. He looks at me and he puts it in my hands because he thinks he's doing a great thing ... because he thinks it's a great thing for me to hold the torch. So I thanked him and I handed the torch back and put it back in the closet.

"And he shows me he burned his arm lighting the torch. Nobody knew that."

Seeing the Opening Ceremony on TV—because of the vast size of the Olympic Stadium while there—Izenberg recalled seeing "sweat coming down his face, and it was hot. But I realize what it is; you know, when he would go to fights at that point, he'd put his hands in his pockets to hide the tremor. ... But he had no pockets in his sweats. ... So he's got his left arm pressed against his body so hard, trying not to shake. And in that concentration, he burned his arm. But he told me about it."

Chapter 11: More Muhammad Ali Memories

The bond between Jerry Izenberg and boxer Muhammad Ali extended beyond their jobs. It was truly unique, far beyond the typical relationships between journalists and pro athletes.

It's 1974, and Izenberg is a recently divorced father. (At the time, Izenberg became the first father in New Jersey to be awarded sole custody of his children, he said.)

He also happened to be doing work in preparation for Ali's fight in Kinshasa, Zaire, against then-world heavyweight champion George Foreman—The Rumble in the Jungle. Izenberg's children, Robert, 11, and Jenny, 8, had just come to live with him two days earlier, so his parental instincts are put to the test.

"I'm driving to Deer Lake (Pennsylvania), and I've got my daughter and my son in the car," Izenberg recalled.

It was a challenging set of circumstances. Izenberg had plenty of work to do. In his heyday, he wrote five columns a week—plus numerous books and magazines articles. And over the years, he was involved in the narration, production and writing of 35 TV documentaries, among them the Emmy Award-nominated "A Man Named Lombardi," about the inimitable NFL coach Vince Lombardi.

En route to Deer Lake, Izenberg is confronted with figuring out how to keep his children occupied while he is covering Ali's training camp.

"He is crazy about television and I'm making a television show at the same time," he remembered about his son, and gave him these instructions: "You can walk around with the crew; they know who you are. Don't worry about it.' "

One down, one to go.

"His (daughter) says, 'What am I gonna do?' " Izenberg recalled.

His orders?

"Well, you go to Aunt Coretta (Ali's paternal aunt) and tell her that you are the official water girl of the Jerry Izenberg television crew and she'll give you a couple of bottles of water and you follow them around, but you keep your mouth shut.

"Then she proceeds to say, 'I hope George Foreman knocks his block off.'

"I said, 'What are you talking about?' "

"I said, 'You've got to remember something: Both of these men are my friends, No. 1. This is a business, No. 2. It's not a war, so they'll do what they do to make their money. And you are going to keep your freakin' mouth shut when you get in there.' "

That set the stage for the TV cameras to get rolling.

"So they go off and do what they do and we do the show," Izenberg said, "and now we are in his locker room and we are talking very softly, and he says to me, 'Is that your son?' "

Ali asked Izenberg what his son's name was, then walked over to him.

"He put his arm around Robert and says, 'Robert, I want to tell you something. You have come to live with a great man who loves you. Learn from him.' And he gets up and walks away," Izenberg remembered.

"Well that's a helluva thing to do for me," he went on. "The kids have been scared. They came to live with me two days earlier."

The conversation continued.

"So is this your daughter here?" The Greatest inquired in a quiet tone.

"When you're 7 years old, 8 years old, tell me what you think we're talking about. She thinks I'm ratting her out about what she said about him," Izenberg pointed out.

"So she's trying to put her shoulders into the molecules in the wall, right? Because she thinks I'm ratting her out."

As Izenberg remembers it, Ali said, "Little girl, will you come up here please. Little girl, I'm talking to you ... You come up here right now!"

Izenberg's daughter walks over to them slowly, and then...

"He swoops down, and he's 6-3, and she wasn't even 5 feet then," the legendary columnist said. "He picks her up and holds her over his head. Now she has lost the total power of English. She cannot speak one word that means anything."

The conversation shifted back to Ali.

"Is that your daddy?" he asked her.

She mumbles.

"Is that your daddy?"

She mumbles again.

"Don't you lie to me, little girl," the boxer said. "Don't you lie to me. That man is ugly. You're beautiful. He's not your daddy. The Gypsies musta brung you. Now give me a kiss right here (he points to his cheek)."

As they're driving home, Izenberg and his daughter begin discussing boxing again.

"She says to me, 'I hope Muhammad can win the fight.' "

Chapter 12: The Power of a Message

Jerry Izenberg's columns, magazine articles, books, TV documentaries and radio appearances have chronicled the lives, accomplishments and challenges of historical figures whose legacies extended far beyond the box scores and annals of sport.

In Major League Baseball, men who endured segregation, racism and death threats and paved the ways for blacks and Latinos in the sport are among the subjects of some of Izenberg's most important (and timeless) work. Jackie Robinson. Larry Doby. Monte Irvin. Roberto Clemente.

Here is a passage from an Izenberg column about Doby from 2012:

"He was as sensitive as he was tough. And, above all, he was tested, perhaps more than anyone I ever knew. Looking back, he was a hero to everyone except himself.

"Historians never really got it. He was the second African-American to play in the majors, the first in the American League. But after Jackie Robinson broke the color barrier with the Dodgers earlier that season, revisionists would have you believe it was all over. This was, after all, America, they reasoned in their footnotes. This was, after all, baseball.

"Doby came to Cleveland six weeks after Jackie had come to Brooklyn. But unlike Jackie, he remained alone for a long, long time. The American League, in contravention to its very name, integrated with the speed of a herniated inchworm.

"Bill Veeck, who may have been the most decent human being ever to own a ballclub, signed him out of the Negro National League, where he played for the Newark Eagles. Their friendship continued right up until Veeck's death years later. They shared a lot - baseball, the game they both loved; late-night jazz, the music to which they listened together on nights when Veeck made surprise visits to whatever city the Indians were in because he wanted to ease the lonely pain that was Doby's only companion that year."

Meanwhile, Izenberg's reporting and on-camera work on Grambling University football coach Eddie Robinson and his team set the standard. He saw what the mainstream media wasn't reporting and opened America's eyes.

During one memorable conversation, Izenberg was asked this: Recalling what you've written about these aforementioned individuals over the years, how important was it to you for your articles to be out there on the sports pages for students to see and for society at large?

"It's very, very important," Izenberg acknowledged.

"Race is a very difficult thing to discuss because everybody has agendas and everybody's afraid. You have to be politically correct. You can't do this, you shouldn't do that.

"On the other hand, I'm not going to be politically correct. Fuck them. I don't care what they think. I don't like those people.

"This is in the minds of so many reporters. ... And I think it goes back to (legendary sports editor) Stanley Woodward. He gave me a lesson, which I didn't even know about when he did it. Later on I heard this story. Most people didn't know it happened."

In 1947, the St. Louis Cardinals had threatened to strike when they came to Ebbets Field to play against the Brooklyn Dodgers and Jackie Robinson, who had broken MLB's color barrier that April.

"A guy named Enos Slaughter, a Hall of Famer I might add, was the guy behind it," Izenberg said, referring to the Cardinals outfielder nicknamed "Country."

Woodward was in his first stint as the New York Herald Tribune sports editor at the time. It was a position of clout, and he learned about the plan hatched by Slaughter and his team.

So what did Woodward do?

He telephoned Ford Frick, the National League president and future commissioner.

"He was really a cipher," Izenberg said of Frick, "much revered by that particular generation of writers because he had been a writer.

"And he said, 'Ford, I'm calling you because I just finished a magazine piece and before I send it off I wanted to tell you about it. It's about the most cowardly president in the history of baseball.' "

Frick was "astonished," Izenberg recalled.

"What are you talking about?" Frick asked Woodward.

Woodward's message to Frick: "You need to suspend that whole fuckin' franchise if you have to. You need to stop this before it starts. If you don't do that, this is going to Look magazine."

Izenberg said that the previous statement was a "bunch of bullshit." But it made a profound impact.

"And if you do stop this thing," he went on, repeating Woodward's words, "I will write about the bravest president we ever had. That's what broke the back of the strike, and nobody ever knew it."

***

Decades ago, Woodward told that story to Izenberg, and it got him thinking...

"We call it the 'toy department,' 'cause it's insignificant, you know? But it ain't," Izenberg declared.

"Nothing is the toy department on a newspaper when people read newspapers. If you know the audience you are trying to reach and you have something important to say ... you've got to say it."

He added: "If it's something of social significance and you know it, you've got to say it. And it's not your personal toy."

The platform given to a columnist cannot be overstated, according to Izenberg.

He followed that point by discussing another famous New York sports scribe, Dick Young.

"I believe Dick Young was the greatest baseball writer who ever lived," Izenberg said, "but he was a mediocre columnist."

He added: "His hatred of (Muhammad) Ali had nothing to do with logic. It had nothing to do with the (U.S.) Constitution. It had nothing to do with a trader or slacker and all that—yeah, that's what he thought because he was a trader, he was a slacker, he was a draft dodger

"Now I don't think I ever would've written that if I had been Dick Young," Izenberg said, noting that Young had received 4-F classification during World War II, which meant he was rejected from military service because of a physical defect.

"But you don't go around telling people to go to a battlefield if you've never been there or at least you weren't eligible to be there. Maybe that's why he was shouting so loud to prove (his masculinity). I don't know his motivation."

Decades later, Izenberg insisted Young made a colossal mistake with the stance he took against Ali.

"You are forfeiting your role as a columnist; now you are becoming an op-ed guy," the Red Smith Award winner stated. "Different thing."

Young, who had a 45-year stint at the New York Daily News, passed away in 1987. And he didn't always see eye to eye with Izenberg.

"One day he was screaming at me, 'It's all bullshit. You're full of shit,' " Izenberg remembered about one heated exchange about Ali.

"And he said, 'Don't tell me about the Constitution. There's a higher law.'

"And I said, 'When I see you come down from Mount Ararat with the tablets, I'll listen to your higher law. Until then, you're full of shit.' "

This heated exchange took place on an airplane.

"At which point the stewardess said, 'If you gentlemen don't sit down and stop the shouting, I'm telling the captain,' " Izenberg recalled.

"But I felt very strongly about it. I think you've got to tell these stories."

Chapter 13: Encounters with Eddie Robinson and Recollections of His First Trip to Grambling

Taking the road less traveled transported Jerry Izenberg to new heights, to the top of his profession.

There were great stories. Everywhere. Including Grambling, Louisiana (pop: 3,144 in 1960).

But first, he had to arrive there to find that out.

Izenberg's first trip to Grambling, and the story behind the story, remains crystal clear in his mind more than 50 years later.

It was 1963, and Roger Kahn, who wrote a critically acclaimed book, "The Boys of Summer," about the Brooklyn Dodgers, worked as sports editor at The Saturday Evening Post. Kahn wanted Izenberg to visit Florida A&M to report on its college football team.

Izenberg had another idea.

"I didn't want to go to Florida A&M because everybody knew that story," Izenberg revealed, "and I was beginning to find out more and more stuff about Grambling."

This was the historically black college where Robinson first coached the football team from 1941-42, then returned in '45 and led the program, uninterrupted, until 1997.

"And nobody even heard of Grambling," Izenberg said, explaining the reality of mainstream America's collective knowledge in the mid-1960s. "So I said, 'Let me go there.' "

"I was," he said, "the first white reporter on the Grambling campus."

He said the university may have had a white teacher then, but he doesn't believe so. The student body didn't have whites.

Which meant he was in a completely different environment than his upbringing in Newark, New Jersey, or in New York City.

"I learned a lot watching Eddie," said Izenberg.

"Eddie was very mistrustful of me when we met. But little things began to happen, and apparently I passed every test."

Such as?

"I was the first guest to stay overnight in the Grambling student center," he said, adding, "When I came down to breakfast the next morning, this whole trip was worthwhile.

"I look at these kids looking at me and I'm saying, 'Now I know what it can feel like.' That's important."

***

Robinson created and maintained an important pipeline from Grambling to professional football. He proved the critics wrong and, in time, opened America's eyes to the talent, athleticism and intelligence of African-American football players. More than 200 of his players were later employed as NFL, AFL and CFL players. He coached future Super Bowl XXII-winning (and MVP) quarterback Doug Williams and Hall of Fame cornerback Willie Brown, as well as wide receiver Charlie Joiner and defensive tackle Buck Buchanan before they launched their distinguished pro careers en route to the Pro Football Hall of Fame in Canton, Ohio.

But before Williams, Brown, Joiner, Buchanan and so many others, Robinson needed a trailblazer to pave the way.

Paul "Tank" Younger signed a contract with the Los Angeles Rams in 1949, making him the first player from a historically black college to sign with an NFL team. Younger played fullback and linebacker for the Rams and Pittsburgh Steelers in a 10-year NFL career. He was selected as an All-Pro four times.

Robinson compiled a record of 408 wins, 165 losses and 15 ties. He amassed 45 winning seasons there. He is No. 2 on the NCAA Division list for coaching victories, trailing only Joe Paterno. Since 1987, the Eddie Robinson Award has been presented annually by The Sports Network to a Division I-AA (now known as the Division I Football Championship Subdivision) top coach.

After the coaching legend's death in 2007 at age 88, the Eddie G. Robinson Museum curated a number of poignant statements about his life and legacy on its website.

Here are two of them:

"Eddie Robinson is a coach's coach. As the son of a legendary coach myself, I saw the greatness in Coach Robinson the minute I shook his hand. When I saw him with his student-athletes, I saw their enormous love and respect for him. When I saw him and Doris together, I saw a lifetime love affair. Coach Robinson is a great leader, father figure, coach, friend, husband, American, and above all, a great human being."

-Richard Lapchick, who co-authored Robinson's autobiography, scholar and civil rights activist

"The coaching profession has lost one of its true legends. Though he was best known for winning more football games than any other coach when he retired, Eddie Robinson's impact on coaching and the game of football went far beyond wins and losses. He brought a small school in northern Louisiana from obscurity to nationwide, if not worldwide, acclaim and touched the lives of hundreds and hundreds of young men in his 57 years at Grambling. That will be his greatest legacy."

-Grant Teaff, executive director of the American Football Coaches Association

***

In a 2004 column about his final visit in Louisiana to see his friend Robinson, who was battling Alzheimer's disease, Izenberg wrote in part: *"Eddie had gotten the Rams to sign Younger, but he had to make the team or the contract was void. If successful, he would be the first player from an all-black school in NFL history. The year was 1949. As they waited there, Robinson put his hands on Tank's shoulders and looked him dead in the eye before he spoke. Then he said: 'Tank, you got to make that*

team. Not just for you, but for all the young black men we can send after you. If you can do that, the door is open to every player in every black college in America. You got to make it. Can you?' And the younger man looked back at him and responded with:

" 'They playin' football, ain't they? If they playin' volleyball, I don't know, coach. But if it's football,' and then he grinned, 'you know I'll make it.'

"He did. All-Pro offense. All-Pro defense ... and hundreds came after him."

In another poignant look at Robinson's legacy from the same column, Izenberg observed: "I thought about the man who always did what was right, who over the years played two white quarterbacks at this all-black college and had a white graduate assistant from New Jersey named Scott Manhoff and didn't give a damn what anybody said because he was a man who never saw color. He is what America should be all about."

***

Postscript: Izenberg's piece on Grambling was rejected by one of the higher-ups at The Saturday Evening Post.

But he didn't give up. He knew he had an important story to tell. So he looked for another outlet to showcase the reporting.

Persistence paid off. True magazine agreed to run it, and the feature ("A Whistle-Stop School with BigTime Talent"), published September 1967, was well-received. E.P. Dutton's annual Best Sports Stories anthology included Izenberg's article.

What's more, Izenberg developed a strong rapport with Robinson, which helped him plant the seeds to write, direct and narrate the ABC documentary "Grambling: 100 Yards to Glory."

Chapter 14: A Rabbi's Influence

Jerry Izenberg's moral backbone, fiber, fortitude, compass—whatever you choose to call it—is directly linked to an important civil rights leader.

While Izenberg grew up in Newark, New Jersey, Dr. Joachim Prinz, a prominent rabbi and civil rights advocate, taught him, and taught him well.

"I was bar mitzvahed by a very famous rabbi, Joachim Prinz," Izenberg said. "Joachim Prinz was a rabbi in Nazi Germany. He got out one step ahead of the knock on the door. He came here and was moved around the country a little bit and then he became the head rabbi at (Temple) B'nai Abraham, which was the largest synagogue in New Jersey, and it was on my block that I lived on.

"And it was where I would get bar mitzvahed," he added, referring to the traditional ceremony and celebration for a Jewish boy on his 13th birthday. This occurred in 1943, during World War II, when the United States was fighting Hitler's Germany.

"His first friends (in Newark) were my mother and father," Izenberg said. "And my father, the old ballplayer, used to listen to the (New York) Giants games every night. And Dr. Prinz would come over and he'd sit with my mother and father on the porch and my father would have the radio on. My mother would be talking to him.

"One night he said to my father, 'Harry, I need a favor,' " Izenberg recalled his rabbi saying. "My father said, 'Not now, not now. (Giants legend) Mel Ott's coming to bat. Wait, wait.'

Mel Ott struck out, prompting Harry Izenberg to blurt out, "What did you want?"

"I want you to teach me baseball," the rabbi said.

"And my father says, 'I didn't know you cared.'

"Dr. Prinz says, 'I don't. But I've got two boys and they're Americans, and I want them to know the game and love it like you do. ... And in return, I'm going to help you with your son Jerry.

"I heard all this because I was in the living room, which is behind the window," Jerry Izenberg disclosed.

Dr. Prinz inquired about the younger Izenberg's preparations for his bar mitzvah. His father said he wasn't sure and admitted he wasn't a regular attendee at the synagogue, "but I'll go to his bar mitzvah and I'll go to my funeral, or my wife's if she goes first."

Upon hearing that, the rabbi issued this order: "Well tell him to come out here and bring his book."

"I should have gone out the back door," Izenberg said more than 70 years later.

He was instructed to chant.

"And my voice is cracking, and my voice is changing, and he says, 'Stop, stop, stop. Another five minutes we'll all be slaves in Egypt again.'

"He turns to my father and says, 'Here's what I'm going to do for you teaching me baseball. I'm going to personally lean on the bar mitzvah teacher to get him ready for this bar mitzvah. I will cancel my vacation. I will bar mitzvah him.'

Admitted Izenberg: "I used to cut that class all the time. After school, I'm playing ball. And, of course, my sister knew exactly where I was playing ball and couldn't wait to rat me out (to the bar mitzvah teacher), who came to the house to say, 'Where is he?' "

She showed them he was at the park, playing baseball. Dr. Prinz was not amused.

"He grabbed me by my ear and pulled me up the street for six blocks. I thought he was a Catholic nun, with a ruler and the knuckles," Izenberg remembered. "And I never missed a class after that.

"And then when Prinz bar mitzvahed me, there were three bar mitzvah boys, me and two others guys whose names I've forgotten. The other two guys could read not one word of Hebrew. Their parents were the biggest donors to the synagogue. You know they were getting bar mitzvahed. So the little kid from up the block had to carry the whole thing in Hebrew, and he wasn't too proficient to begin with."

Later on during the service, Dr. Prinz is preaching to the three boys, who are facing the congregation, and his back is facing the congregation. The rabbi reads out their three names.

"He never looks at the other two ever again because he's promised my father, right? And he's looking at me with those eyes that are burning holes in me, and he says, 'I want you to be an observant Jew, I want you to be a respectful Jew, I want you to be an intellectually curious Jew, and if anybody gives you any crap, I want you to be a fighting Jew.'

"And I'm saying to myself, 'He wants me to be a dead Jew.' "

***

In May 1961, Prinz was among the original Freedom Riders, blacks and whites together, who traveled from Washington, D.C., to the Deep South to protest segregation and demand an end to it at interstate bus terminals. It was organized by the Congress of Racial Equality (CORE).

Mobs of angry whites violently lashed out at the Freedom Riders on their first journey, throwing a bomb in one bus in Alabama and beating Freedom Riders in another with metal pipes, according to contemporary news reports. But this only strengthened their resolve and their cause.

Their fight for equal rights grabbed people's attention at home and abroad.

Subsequent trips took place over the next several months. Hundreds joined the Freedom Riders.

So, looking back, how did Dr. Prinz's involvement in the Freedom Riders grab Izenberg's attention?

"He was on that bus to Alabama, and when he got back out of the hospital—they beat the crap out of all of them—he led part of the congregation over to New York to protest the lunch counter sit-ins in front of the Woolworth Building," Izenberg recalled.

"And that really put me face to face. My parents raised me right in terms of bigotry, but that put me face to face with the fact that it's not enough to be silent.

"Did that affect my writing?" Izenberg reflected. "Well, let's start with the beginning. I'm still a sports columnist, a writer of sorts, and consequently, if this is the story, I'm going to write it. But on top of that, (Dr. Prinz's influence), it wasn't on my mind, but this is the way that I was shaped: You can't be silent either."

In one speech, Prinz declared: "We must never lose sight of the fact that the battle for equality for all people in America is a battle for America."

***

According to published accounts of the March on Washington, before a crowd of 250,000, in August 1963, Rabbi Prinz spoke at the podium after the great Mahalia Jackson sang a gospel tune.

Who spoke next?

Dr. Martin Luther King Jr.

Prinz, who served as president of the American Jewish Congress from 1958 to 1966, talked about discrimination during Adolf Hitler's reign of terror in Nazi Germany.

"When I was the rabbi of the Jewish community in Berlin under the Hitler regime, I learned many things," Prinz was quoted as saying by The New York Times. "The most important thing I learned ... under those tragic circumstances is that bigotry and hatred are not the most urgent problem. The most urgent, the most disgraceful, the most shameful and the most tragic problem is silence."

Dr. King then gave his "I Have A Dream" speech.

***

Years earlier, in 1926 to be precise, Prinz became a rabbi at age 24 in his native Germany. His first book, "Wir Juden" (We Jews), penned in 1933, encouraged Jews to embrace their culture and resist assimilation. He also warned about the rise of Hitler.

"He understood that Hitler was lethal and began early on to urge that Jews leave the country," according to a press kit for the 2013 documentary "Joachim Prinz: I Shall Not Remain Silent. "Thousands took his advice, many thousands stayed and perished in the gas chambers. Life under Hitler was a nightmare. But throughout the next four years, Prinz continued to preach his message and was the subject of numerous arrests and harassment by the Gestapo."

Rabbi Prinz refused to remain silent. And so has Izenberg, using his column to shed light on injustice and corruption, human triumph and tragedy, among other topics through the prism of sports.

Chapter 15: Project Pride

Trying to make the world a better place has been a major focus of Jerry Izenberg's life for decades.

He established a civic organization, Project Pride, in 1979 to make a difference in the community, in the classroom, in sports.

The project grew out of the Red Smith Award winner's pride in his hometown, Newark, New Jersey, and his commitment to social justice.

"I love the city of Newark," Izenberg said. "Now my wife says, 'You're crazy. Now I look what's happening with the shootings and everything.'

"I said, 'That city is dead. But that city is not dead because it's in my mind. For as long as it's in mind, that's what shaped me, that's who I am today. ... It was one of the greatest cities in America, it really was.'"

The July 1967 Newark race riots were the spark that led to the eventual establishment of Project Pride.

"The riots really upset me terribly," Izenberg admitted. "I played ball with black kids, I went to school with black kids, and I had fights with black kids, I had fights with white kids. I fought with everybody. But the point I'm trying to make is that I couldn't understand.

"We had a place called The Mosque (originally named Salaam Temple) here, which the city bought it and changed the name to Symphony Hall (in 1964). A real nice theater, with four levels like Radio City (Music Hall in New York)."

Izenberg recalled that popular black singers would play before sold-out, African-American audiences at the venue. And, he said, "Jerry Vale came to Newark for a concert, sold it out and the audience was all Italian."

That got him thinking.

"I said there's got to be some way to get these people's ass by ass in the same seats," he recalled. "So I said, What do you know? I know sports. I'm going to have a football game. I'm going to have a college football game in Newark every year, it's going to be called the Pride Bowl, and we are going to be a group that calls itself Project Pride.

"I had no idea where the money was going to go, but there were really bad racial tensions then. And we drew 5,000 people to the (first) game. The paper was very cooperative. They let me write and do whatever I wanted to do, put a million stories in.

"And I had an all-black school against Seton Hall University, which has now dropped football. It was going to drop it then and (a school official) said to me, 'Jerry, we're dropping football.'

"I said, 'I've got to have this game. I've got to have this game.'

"He said, 'I'll give you one year.' "

That turned into two years.

Seton Hall, which played its first football game in 1882 against Fordham, played its final varsity season in 1981.

"When we finished, Izenberg went on, "I had Army and Navy junior varsities playing each other—they were called the lightweights—(and) they hadn't gotten bigger to the point, where 175 pounds, you had to weigh that the morning of the game or you couldn't play. But the Army-Navy game was just like any other Army-Navy game."

The Pride Bowl almost became a facsimile of the annual Army-Navy showdown.

"The two super tenants were very good to me," Izenberg said. "They sent me cadets to march, midshipmen to march, the goat, the mule, the cannon, everything. It was like being at the Army-Navy game except you couldn't see it because they only had 8,000 seats."

The Pride Bowl lasted for 29 years.

And with a hint of pride in his voice, Izenberg said: "And we never took a penny from any government funds. The game funded us. We raised $7.5 million in 29 years and, of course, the game program looked like it was bigger than the Super Bowl program. That's where we made the money.

"We started with the $2 ticket and we ended with the $20 ticket, and it was an incredible experience. We had programs that you wouldn't believe."

The Pride Bowl wasn't an immediate financial success. The inaugural game took in $17,000, Izenberg noted, adding, "After that, we were making six figures a game."

"I didn't know what to do with the money," he admitted.

So what happened?

"Project Pride became a conduit into the grammar schools—get the kids early, maybe you can do something," he explained.

"We started an athletic program, which was easy. We had athletes and we had people that wanted to play and we had a million teams. ... But that isn't why we did it. We did it to make respect. We had white kids and black kids on the same team. You had Latinos and whites and blacks playing together."

***

Several years ago, Izenberg spoke to prolific author and boxing columnist Thomas Hauser about Project Pride from its humble beginnings and the difficulty of preparing for (and staging) the first Pride Bowl.

"It was a total nightmare," Izenberg told Hauser for an essay that was included in "Thomas Hauser on Sports: Remembering the Journey."

"I'm a sportswriter, a critic. And all of a sudden, I found myself as a promoter, which was when I began to understand what people who put on sports events go through.

"The game was between Seton Hall and Cheyney State. It rained the entire week. The public transit company refused to add additional buses to the route for the game."

He continued: "Now it's the day of the game. Little kids from local schools are holding up placards with letters on them to spell out cheers, but the kids are standing in the wrong order so the letters are spelling out gibberish. I have parolees from a halfway house blowing up red and blue balloons, but the balloons don't have enough helium in them so they won't lift up. The guy who is supposed to give the signal for the two teams to run out onto the field is having an epileptic fit and is lying on the ground..."

But the hard work paid off. The game became an annual tradition in Newark and did a lot of good for the community. It also created lasting friendships.

"Over the years," Izenberg told Hauser, "the most memorable thing about the games has been what the players take away from them. Each team is adopted by a local high school. The kids from the school interact with the players and some interesting bonds are formed."

More important, the Project Pride academic program sent 1,100 Newark kids to college, with a total of 30,000 students participating in various activities, including remedial reading and cooking.

"We had a girl who wound up on the Harvard AIDS task force," Izenberg said, "where she got her PhD from MIT (Massachusetts Institute of Technology) in biochemistry. We had a program in computers. We had programs in, you name it; whatever the kids seemed to need, we would do.

"I got a guy who was Haitian who taught in the schools and I said, 'Will you teach French to some of my kids?' He said sure.

"I said, 'OK, no Haitians in the class because they can speak French already. We're not going to do that.'

"At the end of each year—he did it for five years—they put on a play in French, these kids who were 11 and 12 and 10, and just like for the hearing-impaired where somebody gets up there and does sign language, I had another kid stand up there and translate every line into English for the kids in the audience.

"We did incredible things with this," he said, proudly. "We were in the Congressional Record. It was just a marvelous experience, and my wife and I were talking about it when it ended and I said, 'If I weren't Jewish, I wouldn't have done this, and that came to the surface about my conversation with the rabbi about Jewish people. And that impacted my life."

He repeated a lesson from his childhood that Rabbi Joachim Prinz, who worked at Temple B'nai Abraham in his hometown, taught him: "We're here for a reason, and the reason isn't us. The reason is to be the best you can be, and being the best you can be also includes the complex sides of our personality."

Izenberg didn't view Project Pride as a cash-making venture. To him, it was the right thing to do.

"You never know what you are touching or who you are touching," he said.

Izenberg said Prinz's values have stayed with him throughout his life.

A rabbi once asked him, "What do you think it means to be a Jew?" Izenberg recalled before reflecting on words of wisdom he learned from Prinz.

"And I said, 'Let me tell you something. You know, they use the word 'chosen' people. I think it's very clear in my mind what it means. It doesn't mean we're better. It doesn't mean we're smarter. It doesn't mean we're His favorites. It doesn't mean anything like that. It means He chose us by giving us the Ten Commandments, which is really essentially what it's all about. And he chose us with a responsibility. Now you've got to make sure, by living that example, you've got to make sure that everybody else knows what it's all about, Jew or non-Jew.' "

***

Then-Congressman Donald M. Payne, a New Jersey Democrat, spoke about the impact of Project Pride before the House of Representatives on Sept. 29, 2003, according to the Congressional Record (Vol. 149, No. 135.)

Payne's speech is printed below.

"*Mr. Speaker, it is with great pride that I rise today to recognize the legendary columnist, Jerry Izenberg, and his immense contributions to the Newark community through his organization, Project Pride.*

"*Jerry Izenberg has been a newspaperman for over 52 years, most recently with the New Jersey Star-Ledger, contributing columns that have appeared throughout the United States, as well as Puerto Rico, Alaska, Mexico, Canada and Italy. As a sportswriter, Jerry Izenberg's accomplishments are incredibly vast. Over his career, he has won numerous literary awards and recognitions, has been inducted into seven Halls of Fame and has been an integral part of the sports world in the United States. To this day, he continues to leave his mark on the sports writing world, all the while inspiring numerous young writers.*

"*And above all, Jerry Izenberg has also managed to be a dedicated family man, with his wife, Aileen, four children and four grandchildren.*

"*Despite all of these remarkable professional and personal accomplishments, I can say with confidence that Jerry Izenberg is most proud of his work with Project Pride. As a native of Newark, New Jersey, Jerry knew of the hardships that the people of that area face on a regular basis. When he founded Project Pride Incorporated 25 years ago, Jerry Izenberg took the personal initiative to create hope and opportunity for the children of Newark. Over the 25 years of its existence, Project Pride has helped send 902 kids to college, allowed the kids in Newark K-5 schools to study a variety of subjects and funded numerous community and athletic programs that have kept as many as 1,000 Newark kids off the streets. What is more amazing, Project Pride has accomplished all of it without accepting a single penny from Federal, State or local funds.*

"*Mr. Speaker, as a member of the Education and Workforce Committee and a former teacher, I understand the significance of the work that Jerry Izenberg has done for the city of Newark. I know that my colleagues here in the U.S. House of Representatives not only join me today in recognizing the tremendous contributions of Jerry Izenberg and Project Pride, but also commending Jerry for his own personal dedication to continue providing the opportunity to so many of our youths.*"

Jerry Izenberg and Red Smith (center) attend a party hosted by NFL Commissioner Pete Rozelle during Super Bowl week in the 1970s. JERRY IZENBERG COLLECTION

Yogi Berra and Izenberg talk at Bears & Eagles Riverfront Stadium in Newark, New Jersey, on the opening night of the Atlantic League of Professional Baseball season in 1999. The Newark Bears played there from 1999 to 2013. JERRY IZENBERG COLLECTION

Izenberg and former NFL coach Bill Parcells at a midtown New York restaurant. The then-Giants coach played a prominent role in Izenberg's inside look at the team in the book "No Medals For Trying: A Week in the Life of a Pro Football Team," chronicling a stretch of the 1989 season. JERRY IZENBERG COLLECTION

Jerry Izenberg at his "office" at Bears & Eagles Riverfront Stadium in Newark, New Jersey, in the early 2000s. JERRY IZENBERG COLLECTION

Izenberg greets Grambling State University coach Eddie Robinson in Grambling, Louisiana, the week before the legendary coach's last game at the helm in 1997. JERRY IZENBERG COLLECTION

Part II

This section features several break-out chapters with more in-depth observations about Jerry Izenberg's career. Prominent writers Dave Kindred, Dave Anderson, Jerry Green and Ira Berkow are among the featured interviewees. Several sources described him as a "national treasure." This section explores that idea and explains why.

Overview

Collectively their insights portray a detailed picture of the broad significance of Jerry Izenberg's career as a giant in sports journalism. A literary giant. Which is why their thoughts and opinions are so vital for this book and for record history.

Some of the elder statesmen in sports media—Anderson, Green, Ira Berkow, John Schulian, George Vecsey and the late Edwin Pope, who spoke to me a few months before he passed away in January 2017 at age 88—and few dozen more contributed their recollections of Izenberg's career and what his career means to them.

Favorite stories about Jerry and, for them, favorite stories he has written are among the topics I asked about. Various viewpoints about his trademarks as a journalist and how he approached his assignments and how he shined on the biggest stage as a writer are among the insights that reached my email inbox or zoomed through my ear drums during phone conversations.

I wanted to find out what journalists thought, and continue to think, about Izenberg's legacy in this business.

There's a clear understanding that Izenberg knows boxing, but you can't overlook his poignant columns on baseball and football and horse racing and much, much more.

But let's return to boxing. He commands attention for his columns and an important 2017 book, "Once They Were Giants: The Golden Age of Heavyweight Boxing," finds him at the top of his game.

In his review of the book for The Sweet Science website, Bernard Fernandez deftly spells out why Izenberg's boxing coverage is important, but also explains how Jerry has thrived as a sportswriter.

"...No comparison of Izenberg to anyone else is valid; like his friend, the late, great Muhammad Ali, the 86-year-old columnist emeritus for the Newark Star-Ledger is an original, a master wordsmith and observer of the human condition who can take familiar source material and wring from it small gems of fresh insight that glisten like diamonds in the noonday sun."

Appropriately, Jerry's ties to Muhammad Ali and boxing were cited by a large number of individuals who were interviewed as obvious trademarks of his career. MLB and NFL tales also filled my notebooks, and general observations about sports journalism from the 1950s to today flowed from the memories of those cited in the pages that follow. And his respect for the written word and passion for storytelling came up again and again and again.

Lengthier tributes to Izenberg and insights about his career are printed below. But first, here are a few, shorter snippets to give you a quick preview:

Pope, an authority on clear, to-the-point prose, summed it up this way: "Jerry always cared about the written word, about making a point in each of his columns."

Robert Lipsyte provided another poignant analyst of Jerry's newspaper columns: "His work should be required reading."

Dave Sims, who calls Seattle Mariners on television, recognizes that Izenberg simply knows how to spin a yarn with the best of them. "Great storyteller," Sims said of Izenberg. "He knows how to read the temperature of people and specifically sports people."

Legendary broadcaster Jim Lampley had this to say about Izenberg's career: "All in all, there was a fundamental integrity and absence of self-consciousness to his work which gave it resonant dignity."

Yahoo Sports boxing scribe Kevin Iole declared: "Of the many thousands of stories written about the death of Muhammad Ali, Jerry's stood tall as easily the best among them."

Former Washington Post sports editor George Solomon: "I consider him one of the giants in the field of sports journalism and stand in awe of his continued prowess as a sports columnist."

Izenberg's longevity in the business, of course, is a recurring theme that popped up in these interviews and in research for this book.

For instance, Steve Politi, a Star-Ledger columnist, penned a tribute to Izenberg on the eve of the 45th Super Bowl.

"Walking around with him the week before the game is like escorting a celebrity down one long red carpet," Politi wrote of Izenberg. "Volunteers stop him. Radio hosts grab him. Izenberg is Super Bowl history, one of the few who can put the behemoth it has become into perspective."

Defiant as ever in 2011 at age 80, Izenberg gave a classic line to Politi that wrapped up the column. And it effectively summed up Jerry's love for the work.

"I look at every Super Bowl as a middle digit pointed up to the sky," he said, "and it's saying, 'Not yet, pal. Not yet.'"

Izenberg became the 20th recipient of the Red Smith Award in 2000 following in the footsteps of the following (in order): Smith, Jim Murray, Shirley Povich, Fred Russell, Blackie Sherrod, Si Burrick, Will Grimsley, Furman Bisher, Edwin Pope, Dave Smith, Dave Kindred, Ed Storin, Tom McEwen, Dave Anderson, Richard Sadler, Bill Dwyre, Jerome Holtzman, Sam Lacy and Bud Collins.

In a profile of Izenberg that ran at the time on the Associated Press Sports Editors website, Politi cited one of his colleague's important crusades decades ago, which was written in 1980 after 18-year-old college freshman fullback Bob Vorhies' death in '77.

"Every important story is not aired incessantly on ESPN," Izenberg was quoted as saying. "I received a letter from the mother of Vorhies, an Irvington, N.J., teenager, who had died in 1977 during punishing workouts at Virginia Tech (known as VPI at the time). "While reporting the story, I found a series of attempts to cover up the death."

Politi noted that Izenberg filed five consecutive columns on the topic, and pointed out it was the only time in his illustrious career that he'd done that.

"It shook me," Izenberg said, looking back. "It taught me that as sports columnists we can do something. I didn't win the case, but I gave (the mother) the ammunition to fight."

In October 1981, the school reached an out-of-court settlement with the Vorhies family, according to published reports. The Vorhies had filed a $14 million lawsuit.

In 2015, Sports Illustrated media reporter Richard Deitsch penned a feature on Jerry Green, Izenberg and Dave Klein, formerly of The Star-Ledger who started an online New York Giants subscription service (the e-Giants newsletter) after 35 years at the paper. They were the three reporters who were covering their 49th Super Bowls.

"At 84, Izenberg drops curses at nearly the same rate he pumped out award-winning columns for The Star-Ledger of Newark before he stepped away from full-time work seven years ago," Deitsch wrote.

"...Izenberg had two spinal operations last year and covering Super Bowl 48 wasn't easy given the cold weather in New Jersey. But he slogged through and he'll be at the big game once again."

For Izenberg, that's always been the plan. And, as a result, countless readers have also come to recognize what Yahoo Sports' Kevin Iole declared a few years ago: "He is a national treasure."

***

Edwin Pope, the late, legendary Miami Herald columnist and 1989 Red Smith Award winner

"Jerry is a great writer. He knows sports. He knows how to tell a story," Pope, who recalled first getting to know Izenberg in the mid-1960s, said in 2016. "It's been a pleasure to meet him many times over the years.

"For decades, he's been one of the best in the business," Pope opined.

< >

Bob Ryan, former Boston Globe columnist, called the "dean of NBA writers" by former commissioner David Stern and 2015 Red Smith Award winner

"I knew Jerry slightly and I enjoyed his company," Ryan stated. "I knew his work and he was a great writer.

"One thing that always dazzles me was that he grew up watching the Newark Bears."

< >

Dave Goren, executive director, National Sports Media Association

"Jerry Izenberg has been as important to American sports media as anyone over the last 60-plus years," Goren said. "A great storyteller with an acerbic wit, Jerry has been one of the premier voices of American sports. If there was an important sports event in the second half of the 20th century, Jerry was there. ... He has truly been a giant in our industry."

< >

Mark Whicker, columnist, Los Angeles Daily News/Orange County Register

"Jerry came from the tradition of two-fisted New York area sports columnists who wrote from the gut and didn't really care how people reacted," Whicker said. "In doing so he got more respect from the people he wrote about.

"He also wrote about social issues because he knew sports wasn't conducted in an isolation booth. And, like all great columnists, he was a reporter first. He shared his knowledge and his good will with those coming up in the business.

"Some of today's newspapers think columnists are an anachronism, but Jerry made people read his paper."

< >

Alex Belth, writer and founder of BronxBanterBlog.com and The Stacks Reader

"I always thought of him as a good guy, yeoman writer, kind of last of a breed in a sense. ... In a way, I think I know more about him as a talking head in documentaries," Belth admitted. "But he is funny, and he goes back to the great, GREAT sports department at the New York Herald Tribune so he's one of those Forrest Gump guys, seen everything and knew everyone."

< >

Richard Lapchick, chair, DeVos Sport Business Management Program, University of Central Florida; director, Institute for Diversity and Ethics in Sport at UCF; Co-Founder, Hope for Stanley Foundation

"I have nothing but great memories about the life and work of Jerry Izenberg of the Newark Star-Ledger," said Lapchick, a noted human rights activist. "He was a long-distance runner as a journalist. His perspectives were always inclusive and he stood tall on ethical issues.

"My dad, (former New York Knicks head coach) Joe Lapchick, admired Jerry enormously. He wrote about my dad's role in integrating sport in America by signing Sweetwater Clifton with the Knicks and reflected on the rivalry between my dad's team, the Original Celtics, and the all-black New York Rens. They played against each other when whites and blacks did not play each other."

Joe Lapchick's respect for Izenberg was introduced to younger generations several years ago. In 2008, Lapchick recalled, "when MSG TV made the documentary 'Lapchick and Sweetwater: Breaking Barriers,' Jerry's voice was loud and clear. I will always remember that he said in the show that 'if I had a son I would want him to play for Joe because he would help him be a better person.' "

He added: "As my own career unfolded with a focus on social issues in sport, Jerry called regularly. He always asked great questions and made me think. He is a national treasure. A great human being."

< >

Sherry Ross, New York metro area-based NHL writer and broadcaster (in 1994, became the first female announcer to work a Stanley Cup Final game, calling it on Radio) and horse racing writer

"Before I became a sportswriter myself, his columns in my local newspaper (the Newark Star-Ledger) were always must-reads for me," Ross said. "One of my favorite sports is thoroughbred horse racing, and he always wrote with passion and humor about the major races, such as the Kentucky Derby. He could always make you feel like you were right there in Louisville.

"In fact, I had never met Jerry until I covered my first Kentucky Derby in 2001. He was very kind and approachable. One thing I noticed about his interviewing style was that he never approached a subject as if he was the expert (a flaw of many columnists). In fact, he often acted as if he was learning about something or someone for the first time, even though he had done his research ahead of time. It is an effective technique. He can tailor his style to any tone that his topic deserves. He is a master storyteller.

"Jerry's sense of right and wrong shines through, especially when he takes a stand for civil rights. He championed Muhammad Ali at a time when it was unpopular, maybe even dangerous to do so."

Ross has a fondness for the influence of Izenberg's upbringing on his life.

"My favorite Jerry Izenberg column is not about a famous athlete or event. Every Memorial Day, the Star-Ledger runs a column he wrote about his immigrant father Harry," Ross said. "Harry Izenberg served in World War I and worked grueling hours in a dye factory, an occupation that probably shortened his life. Yet he made sure his young son learned to play and love the sport that was emblematic of his adopted country: baseball. And from that beginning, Jerry Izenberg carved out a career his dad could never have dreamed of. Every year the column runs, and every May I take the time to read every unchanged word."

Izenberg didn't have to toot his own horn to earn respect from his peers.

"As to why Jerry Izenberg isn't more 'famous,' I can't answer that," said Ross. "Maybe because he seldom made himself the focus of his story, or took up some ludicrous position just to get attention, or insulted people or acted like a jerk."

<>

Jim Lampley, boxing play-by-play announcer, 2015 International Boxing Hall of Fame inductee and broadcaster who worked at 14 Olympic Games

"First off, I think it is fair to place Jerry within a select group of American sports reporters who rolled back the curtain of romantic mythification which had enveloped sports for decades prior to their arrival, and gave to readers and listeners a new unvarnished version of the competitive sports world which was even more compelling than its predecessor because it had the power of truth," Lampley commented. "I would call them the social realists, and the list would include people like Howard Cosell, Dick Schaap, Larry Merchant, Jim Murray, Jim McKay and various others whose careers meshed with the Civil Rights Movement, the Vietnam War, and other complementary forces which gave energy to that transformation. Jerry is unquestionably a part of all that.

"As your questions establish, there is a particularly strong link to race, and to figures like Muhammad Ali and Eddie Robinson and Jim Brown who helped upend behavioral stereotypes and make clear the sports world would be an active adjunct to progress. Jerry was one of the best at understanding their message and giving them a voice.

"There is no question he would have had greater overall impact in the interactive landscape of today, where if your work is distinctive the web will give it national exposure, than in the world in which the Newark Star-Ledger was a lesser platform than the New York or Los Angeles papers. But if you knew what you were looking for you knew it was important to read him, so plenty of the right people did. And smarter young reporters understand the validity of paying him homage on press row, and they do it.

"All in all, there was a fundamental integrity and absence of self-consciousness to his work which gave it resonant dignity. I like to tell him he is what Cosell would have dreamed he was if he weren't so busy making sure to be heard. Howard was a very serious sports reporter who was intensely interested in being recognized for it. Jerry is just a very serious sports reporter. It's enough, in this business, to make him immortal. I am just honored he recognizes me and seems to enjoy it when I walk over to say hello."

< >

Cormac Gordon, former columnist, Staten Island Advance

"Jerry Izenberg's body of work over more than a half century speaks for itself in terms of his ability to tell a story, to shine a light into dark places, to give voice to people who couldn't be heard," Gordon reflected.

"In my mind he has never been a sportswriter or even a journalist so much as a crusader and a moralist. His consistent championing of the sports heroes (known and unknown) of black America might be his most important legacy."

This included the Newark Bears, Eddie Robinson, (Larry) Doby, Monte Irvin, (Don) Newcombe and Jackie Robinson.

Gordon said Izenberg's work with the Newark public school system and with Project Pride and the Pride Bowl stands out as a crowning achievement of his life.

"In terms of Triple Crown (races), Super Bowls, etc, he was always an entertaining deadline-writing columnist who came to work early and stayed late," Gordon said. "As someone who often sat next to him in the leaky basement of the old Yankee Stadium on playoff and World Series nights into the 2000s I can attest to the fact that he still had the juice and the desire to make it happen under pressure."

Gordon saw firsthand that Jerry took pride in every column he crafted, never in a rush to get it done quickly.

"I was with Jerry in Atlanta's old ballpark (Atlanta-Fulton County Stadium) one night for a Mets playoff game when he would not leave until he got the final piece of his column just right," Gordon recalled.

"We got locked inside the ballpark."

What happened next?

"I had to climb a fence to get out, then find a security guard to open the gate to let Jerry out," Gordon said.

"I think he's still like that today at 86. It's amazing to me."

< >

Tom Verducci, Sports Illustrated senior baseball writer, MLB Network insider and TBS reporter

"I grew up in Essex County delivering The Star-Ledger and reading Jerry," Verducci said. "I once took a high school elective on honors Mythology because I told my advisor I wanted to be a writer and he made note of how Jerry would sometimes reference Greek mythology.

"Jerry's writing was made more impactful by his community involvement. Newark and its people were closer to his heart than sports. My father was born and raised in Newark and went on to become a high school Hall of Fame football and baseball coach. So Newark, the Ledger and Jerry all occupied a special place in my consciousness as an aspiring writer.

"Jerry and Steve Jacobson (formerly of Newsday) always have been hidden gems in the sportswriting world, lacking the recognition to match their talent and enterprise."

< >

Michael Socolow, media historian, author of "Six Minutes in Berlin: Broadcast Spectacle and Rowing Gold at the Nazi Olympics" and director, McGillicuddy Humanities Center Communication & Journalism, University of Maine

"I'd always thought of Izenberg as the raconteur you see in the Ali documentaries—but your interviews with him made me aware that he was the last of the great sports columnists to work under Stanley Woodward at the New York Herald Tribune—widely considered the greatest sports editor ever," Socolow said.

"He really is the last of the breed—guys like Jimmy Cannon, Paul Gallico, and Frank Graham—who covered everything while developing their own style and voice. I'm not sure newspapers can afford this anymore."

< >

James Fiorentino, New Jersey-based portrait artist and illustrator

"Jerry is a legend in sportswriting and in New Jersey," Fiorentino said. "He has experienced and written about some of the biggest moments in sports history and there is no doubt he is underrated because of where he has been at all these years. He has his own unique style like most great writers and I was honored to have him write about me some years ago and still will mention my 25th anniversary Triple Crown painting (Affirmed vs. Alydar, in 1978) I had done when he talks about the Triple Crown in his columns.

"I feel very lucky that he wrote for the Star-Ledger all those years and he is a part of sports history for sure. To me, a Hall of Famer!"

< >

Dave Sims, Seattle Mariners TV play-by-play announcer, NFL radio announcer for Westwood One

"I love Jerry. Smart, tireless, passionate, insightful," Sims said. "He was one of my all-time great guests when I was doing the early days of what is now known as radio row during the 1987 and 1988 Super Bowls. Great storyteller. He knows how to read the temperature of people and specifically sports people."

< >

Martin "Marty" McNeal, former longtime Sacramento Kings beat writer, Sacramento Bee

"I grew up watching, looking forward to seeing Jerry on Sunday night's 'Sports Extra,' " remembered McNeal, in a 2018 interview. "Rarely missed it. Jerry's segment always was powerful, real and best of all, him. I just was a fan with no thoughts of becoming a journalist.

"When I became one, it was a highlight to meet him and he immediately gave respect to a young black man for no reason whatsoever," added McNeal, who passed away in 2020. "I realized he was special from the brief interaction as well as his writing, which was different than everyone else's."

< >

Bob Papa, longtime radio voice of the New York Giants, Golf Channel announcer

"As a kid growing up in New Jersey, Jerry's column was a staple of my youth," Papa admitted. "He had a way of drawing you into his column with a lead that made you think.

"My television career began in 1989 in the world of boxing. It was an amazing experience getting to know Jerry. Talking the 'fight game' with him at a big fight weigh-in was a treat. Jerry has a way of using history to bring the present to light.

"I have also interviewed him about the history of the Super Bowl. He was there from the beginning. His stories are amazing, but he NEVER speaks down to you.

"Jerry, like his columns, invites you into his stories. He is a true national treasure. A pro's pro but a gentleman first."

< >

Neil Best, sports columnist, Newsday

"As someone who did not grow up reading Jerry in his heyday—because I was reading Newsday on Long Island—my most vivid Jerry memories from my teenage years were his essays on 'Sports Extra' on Channel 5 on Sunday nights," Best remembered. "They were state of the art for their era. I particularly remember the one he did on the demolition of an old ballpark. Maybe it was Roosevelt Stadium in Jersey City."

He added: "Jerry clearly was an important historical figure in late 20th century sports, notably in his unheralded role as a defender of Muhammad Ali. He was/is fearless when it comes to social issues and advocating for them."

Has Jerry been overlooked in the 21st century?

"I think that's probably true," Best said. "But most savvy sports fans in the New York area—especially those of a certain age—understand and appreciate the value and importance of his work and career."

< >

Patrick Farabaugh, associate professor of communications, St. Francis (Pa.) University, author, St. Francis football and basketball play-by-play announcer. (Izenberg wrote the foreword for his book, "An Unbreakable Bond: The Brotherhood of Maurice Stokes and Jack Twyman.")

"Jerry Izenberg is a prolific sportswriter and a legend on the American sportswriting scene," Farabaugh. "Yes, he churns out bylines, but his work is good stuff. To have written as much as he does while simultaneously maintaining a high level of quality is remarkable.

"He has a unique style—his writing has wit and an edge, sprinkled with wisdom and warmth. The stars aligned for The Star-Ledger when it hired Jerry Izenberg 65 years ago and sports fans have been blessed with his writing ever since."

<>

Bill Dwyre, 1996 Red Smith Award winner, former Los Angeles Times sports editor and columnist

"Jerry's newspaper career has been in the East, mine in the Midwest and West," Dwyre said. "That being said, I always knew who he was and had a great deal of respect for him. And more recently, when I began a second career as a sports columnist at the LA. Times, after 25 years as the sports editor there, I got to know Jerry very well. We both did lots of columns on boxing.

"My favorite thing about Jerry was that he never got tired, he never stops looking for stories."

Dwyre provided a good example that illustrates Jerry's quest to find compelling stories.

"We both were at a news conference recently when the subject of a young boxer named Jose Ramirez began to be discussed," Dwyre said. "Ramirez was not only a boxer, but a former farm field worker in the Central Valley of California. As such, he has not turned his back on his former life and the people in it. He now uses his boxing celebrity as a vehicle to call attention to the water-rights plight that is facing the Central Valley and the importance of that to his family, friends and a large part of the world that is fed by the Central Valley. Many of us wrote columns about it. So did Jerry.

"Then, the next time I saw him, he said he had been so taken by Ramirez's story that he was going to carve out time to go to the Central Valley, talk to a bunch of people and write a book. The rest of us saw the story as 800 words. Jerry saw a book. In retrospect, Jerry was right.

"That is the essence of Jerry Izenberg."

(Izenberg later revealed, however, that he's not pursuing a book on Ramirez due to the time he would need to complete the project.)

<>

Dick Weiss, former Philadelphia Daily News and New York Daily News sportswriter specializing in college football and college basketball. He now writes for BlueStar Media.

"He was a huge advocate of the Civil Rights Movement and is beloved in (Newark)," Weiss said. "One of the most principled, courageous writers in the history of sports journalism. very old school New York/North Jersey journalist who wasn't afraid to take on any issue. He had the best feel for all things New Jersey of any writer I've dealt with. Coaches and players feared and respected him. He rarely was off point when he wrote his column. I was sad to see him leave the profession (full time). I thought he would do this forever.

"As a young writer, I considered him a giant in the metropolitan area. Later on when I worked in New York, I really looked forward to seeing him at big college events."

<>

Kevin Iole, boxing and mixed-martial arts columnist, Yahoo Sports

"Jerry Izenberg is one of the true giants of the industry and deserves to be spoken of in the same league as legends such as Red Smith and Jim Murray," Iole said. "He is a beautiful writer who has an extraordinary way with words, but he has a knack for getting to the heart of a matter. He finds the stories others missed."

For Iole, Izenberg's gift for rising to the occasion for the most difficult assignments has not gone unnoticed.

"Of the many thousands of stories written about the death of Muhammad Ali, Jerry's stood tall as easily the best among them," Iole said. "Izenberg was never afraid to take a stand, and he backed Ali at a time when it wasn't popular to do so. Ali, as a result, gave Izenberg access and insights that he gave few others, and Jerry was able to present a robust, full picture of the man at the end of his life.

"He was an extraordinary journalist for decades, but even in retirement, in his 70s and 80s, his work remains stellar. He is a true national treasure and the standard by which many others who follow will be judged."

< >

Ivan Maisel, college football reporter, ESPN

"Jerry is important to journalists in the same way that Vin Scully is important to the Dodgers," Maisel commented. "He has always been there, a lighthouse on the shore. I admire his sense of right and wrong and his passion in delivering it to you in such clean prose. Some writers get stale with age. I didn't get that sense with Jerry.

"I haven't read a lot of Jerry through the years. I just didn't see his stuff that often. But I have an anthology that includes a piece he did on Zoilo Versalles, the Twins' second baseman for most of the '60s. What struck me about that was the clarity of his prose, how descriptive he was in one sentence. The premise alone of the story was good: a young guy in bad weather a long way from home. Jerry had good story ideas, a skill that is really underrated."

< >

George Vecsey, retired New York Times sports columnist and author

"Jerry Izenberg is one of those insider sports columnists from the time of Jim Murray and Jimmy Cannon to the time of Christine Brennan and Sally Jenkins," Vecsey noted.

"I would see him at the big-people table at the Kentucky Derby or the Super Bowl, a regular. I know he's written about Ali and Lombardi and Mantle—but the thing I like most about Jerry is that he is a Newark guy. He has never lost it, never forgotten.

"Every year he would remind me of the Pride Bowl he helped run, to raise scholarship money for young people from Newark. He would rave about the great colleges—Army, Navy, Ivy League schools—that send their sprint football teams, their bands, their cheerleaders, their aura—to Newark.

"To my everlasting shame, I never got over there for the Pride Bowl, but I loved his pride in the people in his hometown.

"It was not the kind of thing you hear much in press boxes. We write about other people's good deeds but we're usually on the road when good deeds are being done. Jerry has never left Newark, in his heart. That's really big-time."

< >

Peter Vecsey, legendary pro basketball scribe and TV pundit

"I spoke to him once in my life, at Larry Doby's funeral," Vecsey recalled. "We discussed a player who had spit, I believe, at Larry during a game. Maybe much more than that. Doby, who said very little, had told me about the incident at a (former New Jersey Nets owner) Joe Taub dinner we regularly attended. I thought I was privy to the name. Jerry used the name when discussing the incident. It demonstrated how trusted he was. By many athletes."

During another discussion about Izenberg and Doby, Vecsey added this comment: "It was clear Jerry was a trusted confidant."

< >

George Solomon, former Washington Post sports editor and former director of the Shirley Povich Center for Sports Journalism at the University of Maryland. The 2003 recipient of the Red Smith Award.

"Jerry Izenberg was an exceptional columnist who always had the feel for the right column, the most interesting issue of the day and a great view of sports and the world," Solomon said. "As important, he knew his readers and knew what they wanted to read. He also was never afraid to go against the tide.

"I consider him one of the giants in the field of sports journalism and stand in awe of his continued prowess as a sports columnist."

<>

Robert Lipsyte, author, TV correspondent, former New York Times sports and city columnist, ex-ESPN ombudsman. He wrote the memoir "An Accidental Sportswriter."

"Jerry is an enormously influential sports journalist on a number of levels," Lipsyte declared. "And it's true that he may not have gotten the mass national audience he deserved because the Newark Star-Ledger is not a national paper. But his extensive and pioneering TV work, particularly around Grambling and Lombardi, gave a perspective on those subjects that informed all journalism to come on the subjects. In that sense, so did his columns.

"Jerry was already well-established when I came on the scene in the early Sixties. I'm grateful for his generosity to a younger sportswriter—more important, I, like many others, read his columns consistently and carefully for information and for opinion. Jerry was far more progressive, open-minded and forward thinking than most sportswriters of his time and ready to put his attitudes into practice—consider his charitable good works in Newark.

"On the ongoing topics of his era—for example, Muhammad Ali and the growth of pro football into America's new pastime—Jerry was amazingly clear-eyed at the least, often searingly skeptical. I think those qualities never left him. As an old man in the 21st century, he added history and wisdom to his tools of choice."

In Lipsyte's view, Izenberg's brilliance and importance in his chosen profession go hand in hand.

"There is no question in my mind that Jerry has been one of the best and most important sportswriters of my time," Lipsyte offered. "His work should be required reading."

<>

John McClain, longtime NFL writer (more than 40 seasons), Houston Chronicle, who joined the newspaper in 1976.

"Jerry is an icon whose popularity transcends sports," McClain stated. "He's been so good for so long that he's earned respect and admiration in and out of the sports world. He's been a terrific example for so many of us who have followed his career, whether it be up close or, in my case, from afar.

"Jerry is a true journalist, a sports columnist who can make you laugh or cry. You may not always agree with him, but he always informs and entertains his readers. He's been prolific as a columnist and author of sports books for decades.

"Jerry always conducts himself in a professional manner. He can skewer or praise, but he's always fair, and that's why he has so much credibility and respect with his readers and fellow journalists. Jerry is one of the all-time greats who should be in that sportswriting pantheon that includes the true legends of our business."

<>

Thomas Gerbasi, editorial director for UFC and a longtime boxing reporter

"If I had to pick one trait of Jerry's that I love the most, it's that he's always let the work speak for itself," Gerbasi said. "He wasn't trying to be a multimedia rock star like so many in this business. He doesn't have a regular gig on ESPN, he doesn't have a Twitter account (at least I don't think he does), and he isn't screaming at the universe on a weekly podcast. So yeah, he's overlooked these days, but that's the case for a lot of the greats. I wonder if the new generation of boxing writers even knows who guys like Jerry and (Michael) Katz are. That's unfortunate because when I started doing this—1996—there was no social media, the Internet was still in its early stages, and when I was around guys like them, I sat down, shut up and listened. These were gods to me, and I don't think the younger generation appreciates the written word like it used to. Jeez, I sound like I'm 90, but at 48, I'm getting there. But to answer the question, I think Jerry has been overlooked because he's not out there screaming 'LOOK AT ME!' "

When the discussion of Izenberg's top traits as a journalist came up in discussion, Gerbasi didn't hesitate to share his thoughts.

"The first thing that comes to mind is how he took me to places I had never been, introduced me to people I never met, and showed me things I never saw with my own eyes. If a writer can do one of those things, he or she is pretty special," Gerbasi shared. "To do all three, that shows you how good Jerry is."

And what's the hallmark of his columns?

"I think it was A.J. Liebling that said a good fight report should be like a letter to a friend," Gerbasi said. "That's what Jerry provides. You always got a personal touch along with the nuts and bolts of the story. He never tries to impress you with his vocabulary and the greatest compliment I can give him is one I received once: you don't need a thesaurus next to you in order to enjoy the story."

< >

Greg Bishop, senior writer, Sports Illustrated

Bishop looked back on what it was like just starting out in this business at the same paper where Izenberg was an icon.

"Before I wrote for The New York Times or Sports Illustrated, or even The Seattle Times, I interned at The Star-Ledger in 2002," Bishop said. "It was summer, I was nervous and here's why: that staff. Steve Politi and Brad Parks writing takeouts. David Waldstein on the Mets, Dan Graziano on the Yankees, Dave D. (D'Alessandro) covering the NBA and the Knicks. But there was only one guy who made my hands shake when I met him, and that was Jerry Izenberg.

"I was 22 years old. I knew nothing. Jerry had been writing columns forever. He knew everything. He wrote about boxing and the NFL and horse racing and baseball. And it wasn't just columns, not just opinions, or hot takes. The words he laid out on the page were closer to poetry than narrative. He had so many great analogies, comparisons that made you think you weren't watching the same game, that he was processing what happened on a deeper, more critical level than you were capable of. He reminded me (a journalism nerd, at heart) of Red Smith, or Jim Murray, and he belongs, in my humble opinion, up there with them on whatever Mount Rushmore of sportswriters might exist.

"The best part is he's still writing. He writes more than I do and better and with more verve. Writers like Jerry Izenberg don't come around too often, but I'm personally glad they do. I've only met Jerry Izenberg a few times; I doubt he'd even remember. But I learned a lot from reading him that I use every day. And I'm sure I'll learn something from whatever column he writes next."

< >

Wayne Coffey, the author of more than 30 books, including "The Boys Of Summer" about the 1980 U.S. Olympic ice hockey team. He worked for the New York Daily News for more than 30 years.

"My enduring image of Jerry is a little man with a goatee, a raspy voice and an unstinting passion for writing with a freshness, humor and startling insight—again and again and again," Coffey said. "Probably no other columnist in history has been more prolific, or more consistently superb, or more spirited when it came to taking on hypocrisy and injustice.

"We're all richer for having been Jerry Izenberg's journalistic brethren."

< >

Christine Brennan, USA Today columnist. She became the first president for the Association of Women in Sports Media in 1988.

"He's a wonderful writer and a legend in our business, and it's always an honor to be in the same press box with him," Brennan remarked.

< >

Nancy Cantor, chancellor, Rutgers University-Newark (Izenberg's alma mater)

"I think that the most remarkable thing across all of Jerry's accomplishments is that through it all, with all of the close connections he's had to so many of the greatest athletes of all time, he maintains great humility and continues to want to turn the spotlight toward others," Cantor said.

For Canton, among the most memorable times interacting with Izenberg in recent years involved talk of his beloved hometown.

"I was having lunch with Jerry not long ago and we were talking about his love for his hometown, Newark, and his alma mater, Rutgers University-Newark, and how people from every background imaginable (which really reflects sharply the diversity of our region in North Jersey) find their opportunity—educational opportunity—to make it in this world at our institution," Cantor said.

"And it struck us that Jerry really represents exactly that for his generation—a generation that grew up in Newark when it was a bustling industrial hub full of first- and second-generation Americans, largely from different countries than today's new arrivals, but deeply determined to make the most of their talents while making a difference in the world.

"That is Jerry. And he is deeply committed to helping our new generations of strivers to succeed."

In conclusion, Cantor stated that Jerry's ever-present empathy, his respect for the hardships that people overcome, is a redeeming quality.

"Jerry's profound respect for people who face tremendous challenges seems to be there behind everything he does," Cantor said. "Not only is it in the highest-profile people he's written about, like Muhammad Ali, but it's there in his admiration for athletes like an Olympic wrestler who battled cancer en route to a gold medal."

<>

Pat Borzi, sportswriter for MinnPost.com, the author of "Minnesota Made Me," which was released in November 2018, and a former colleague at The Star-Ledger.

"I bought one of his early books when I was in grade school," Borzi remembered. " 'Championship,' a history of NFL Championship games and the early Super Bowls, came out around 1968. That's when sports suddenly interested me for the first time. Growing up on Long Island, I was one of those kids who grabbed every book about baseball, football and basketball I could get my hands on, either at the library or through Scholastic Books at school. Most of the big-name New York-area writers turned out quickie sports books, and I read most of them, but that one always stuck with me. Jim Brown was on the cover, if memory serves.

"Many years later, when The Ledger hired me to cover the Yankees and I got to read Jerry all the time, I understood and appreciated the things that attracted me to his writing in the first place. Jerry writes with vivid color. He puts you in the seat next to him. You can see the punches, hear the crowd, smell the popcorn and the stale cigars. He gives you just enough so you can fill in the rest. And Jerry can tell a story as well as anybody in the business. Now that I've known him for 20-plus years, whenever I read one of his columns, I can hear his gravelly voice in my ears—minus the f-bombs, of course.

"And that brings me to Jerry's other great gift—he can sniff out bullshit in a heartbeat. You can't get at the truth without sifting through deception, and few navigate deception as well and as fearlessly as Jerry.

"Most of all, Jerry is as down-to-earth and genuine a guy as I've ever met in the business. I'm honored to have worked with him, and even more honored to know him as a friend. He'll probably have something clever to say about that, too."

<>

Keith Olbermann, longtime broadcaster for ESPN and other media outlets

"It always struck me that he signed off his WNEW-TV reports with 'This has been Jerry Izenberg for Sports Extra.' It was such a strange use of tense, a writer sacrificing the moment of filming for the moment of viewing. Reminded me of Waite Hoyt doing his play by play in the past tense," Olbermann stated. "And of course if it were ever said with the wrong inflection it would have been the fully self-abnegating 'this has-been, Jerry Izenberg.'"

<>

Charley Steiner, former "SportsCenter" anchor for ESPN, current Los Angeles Dodgers play-by-play announcer

"Jerry was a street smart and savvy columnist, with a great sense of humor," Steiner said. "He was a quintessential 'Jersey guy' and that made his writing especially effective. His writing had an edge to it. He understood the streets and those who came from them, because he did. During his heyday, the New York journalistic community was populated by some of the great writers/communicators of all time. Red Smith, Dave Anderson, Dick Young, etc. and Jerry was a proud and standing member."

Steiner went on: "I spent a fair amount of time covering many of the stories that he did, especially boxing. One of things I remember and admired most about Jerry was his love, affinity, and respect for the African-American community. It was real and passionate and genuine. I too had a good relationship with Ali, but nowhere near as close as Jerry had. We would often compare notes and thoughts about Ali, who remains to this day the athlete and person I most admired. The fact that Ali allowed Jerry into his sparsely populated inner circle, speaks volumes about Jerry's intellect, sensibilities, passion and compassion."

In conclusion, Steiner delivered a huge compliment to Izenberg.

"Jerry Izenberg was an 'ink-stained wretch'... a newspaperman's newspaperman. When newspapers really meant something," Steiner said.

Part II
Chapters

"There's clarity and there's depth in his writing, and I think he's very analytical."
-Jerry Green

More than most, Jerry Green knows the significance of the totality of Jerry Izenberg's sportswriting and his career as a whole.

Green and Izenberg were the only two newspaper columnists to cover the first 51 Super Bowls.

A fraternity of two.

Remarkable.

"We share a survival instinct," said Green, who has written for the Detroit News for decades. "He's a survivor, I'm a survivor, and I appreciate the fact we're both interested in each other continuing to cover (sports) because we represent an era that is long gone in American sports media. We covered national events and it would make some sort of reputation for ourselves."

Clearly, Izenberg was in the right place at the right time early in his career with Stanley Woodward, the New York Herald Tribune sports editor as his legendary mentor, according to Green. And Woodward was a big part of those formative years.

"He came up with a terrific pedigree in that he had associations that other writers lacked being out of the New York area," Green said of Izenberg.

Green gave an example of Izenberg's important connections, noting his close ties to NFL Commissioner Pete Rozelle, the subject of his 2014 book, "Rozelle: A Biography."

"He really got to know people in depth and a lot about them, and he was able to put that into words," Green said

Green believes he first met Izenberg at the 1966 NFL Championship Game at the Cotton Bowl in Dallas, where the Cowboys took on the Green Bay Packers. The Packers led 14-0 en route to a 34-27 on Jan. 1, 1967.

Izenberg "had a closeness to (Hall of Fame coach Vince) Lombardi that I did not have because he coached on the New York Giants staff there before he went to Green Bay," Green said.

***

Like Dick Schaap, Izenberg also saw the rise of civil rights as an issue of profound importance in the 1960s, and sports was not immune to societal changes that focused on civil rights. Izenberg's support of Muhammad Ali's right to refuse to serve in the U.S. military during the Vietnam War on religious grounds set him part from the vast majority of his newspaper peers.

"He was in Ali's camp right from the beginning, I would say, from the time Cassius Clay changed his name," Green said.

With decades spent reading and writing what appears on the sports pages of American newspapers, Green developed a deep understanding of what has made Izenberg an effective sportswriter.

"There's clarity and there's depth in his writing," Green said, "and I think he's very analytical."

Green's nimble mind unearthed a classic example from Super Bowl II: Izenberg's reporting on an "in-the-trenches showdown" between Packers offensive guard Gale Gillingham and Raiders defensive tackle Tom Keating. As Izenberg watched the action unfold before his eyes, the combatants on opposite sides of the line of scrimmage became a compelling slice of the game's overall drama, according to Green.

"He got into that," Green said of Izenberg's analytical writing, "just the way they beat up on each other. He talked to both of them ... and I don't think there was any other sportswriter in America at that time in those early years (of the Super Bowl) who would do something like that.

"Jerry was able to pick up this battle in the trenches, providing a fresh perspective on one of the game's pivotal matchups."

Other journalists focused on Green Bay quarterback Bart Starr or Lombardi's last game as Packers coach or running back Jim Taylor or the NFL's dominance of the AFL, Green recalled. Izenberg's coverage set him apart from the masses.

To this day, "he has perception," Green stated.

In February 2018, Izenberg and Green sat side by side in the press box for Super Bowl LI in Houston, watching the New England Patriots and Atlanta Falcons.

"I knew he was interested in the fumble, which actually was the turning point in the game," Green said, referring to Patriots linebacker Dont'a Hightower's sack of Falcons quarterback Matt Ryan in the fourth quarter that sparked a remarkable comeback by New England. At the time of the turnover, Atlanta led 28-12.

A key section of Izenberg's game column focused on the pivotal play.

Here's a portion of it: *"It was third-and-one on the Falcons' 36 and here came Hightower from his linebacker position, the honest workman doing his job. He zeroed in on Ryan, who—inexplicably to some—had dropped back to throw. Hightower came on like an avenging angel or a giant eraser, determined to wipe clean the earlier mistakes of the embarrassed Patriots.*

"The linebacker arrived so ferociously, it was almost a dead heat between him and the shotgun snap, which he jarred loose as Ryan went down. The Pats recovered.

"He hadn't lit a spark. He had ignited a full-scale forest fire. Brady threw four straight completions, starting at the Falcons' 25 and ending with Danny Amendola cradling the football in the end zone. A two-point conversion kept the flame alive.

"But for all the scoring in this game, it was Hightower who got it going and now there was no coping with the Real Patriots."

Green penned a more traditional column with a piece about Pats QB Tom Brady.

***

So when did Green begin to understand that Izenberg possessed a special talent to write about sports?

"The first thing that I really got to admire Jerry for was he came out with a book called 'The Rivals,' " Green said of his colleague's 1968 book. "It really captured the flavor of sports," he went on," which Jerry always did. He could capture the flavor of a game and games."

Others agreed.

Citing the Joe Louis-Max Schmeling fistic rivalry, Notre Dame-Army football, Sea Biscuit vs. War Admiral, among others, Izenberg delivered a first-rate treatise on American sports.

Summing up the book, here's the Kirkus review: "With a jovial good humor and a delicate regard for the behavioral eccentricities of athletes under fire, Mr. Izenberg recalls, in a lively and original style, tournament traumas of the not-too-distant past. Classy showing on a well-run track."

Izenberg demonstrated how to use a wide range of cultural and historic references to complete the task.

"Mr. Izenberg decorates his combat commentaries with delectably apt quotes—from Job and Ralph Waldo Emerson to Alfred Shotgun Foley," Kirkus stated.

One book, of course, didn't cement Izenberg's legacy in journalism, but it gave a glimpse into what he's able to do in this arena of human (and equine) drama.

"I think he's prolific and I would say he is a national sportswriter, and the way our business is going we don't have that many anymore, so he's a throwback to the Red Smith era," said Green, who served as a U.S. Naval press officer in Asia in the 1950s before returning to New York and, in '56, pursuing a career in journalism. In 1955, Green penned a column on a Sugar Ray Robinson fight that he had listened to on the radio while stationed in Japan, then distributed the column at the Foreign Correspondents' Club of Japan in Tokyo. The Asahi Evening News, a now-defunct English-language newspaper, printed the column.

"The first time I read Jerry Izenberg he was working for the New York) Herald Tribune (from 1958-62), so he was working with Red Smith," Green said.

Describing that era's prominent talent, Green said the group of distinguished journalists included Jimmy Cannon and Jack Murphy.

"They were older than Jerry and I were, but we would look at them and admire them and ... try to emulate them."

It worked.

"I would say maybe he's the 21st century Red Smith," Green commented.

In his own right, fueled by his work ethic, talent and intellect, Izenberg made a name for himself in sportswriting.

"I would go to an Ali fight or a Super Bowl and realize that he is one of the icons in our fading business," said Green.

***

Green wasn't shy about pointing out why he and Izenberg continue to concoct relevant columns, even as they move closer to their 90th birthday.

"One of the best things about him and myself is we have a perspective of history," Green stated, "and we can take current events such as the Super Bowl and go out and write about Vince Lombardi and bring it up to the current situation."

What's more, Izenberg's all-around abilities as a journalist turn his prose into a work of art.

Being a skillful observer of every detail in front of him, including how and what is said in individual and group settings, helped propel Izenberg to the top of his profession.

"Yes, he was able to pick out statements and dramatize them and analyze them and use that analysis directing him to the game's final outcome, which is a rare ability," Green said. "It takes special insight as a journalist to be able to do that.

"He has superior insight to other sportswriters and sports columnists of our era," added Green. "He's a serious journalist, the kind of journalist you're supposed to be, and few people attain that level of competence that he has plus for the output that he has had.

"I'll say this: He's ambitious because he's still writing books deep into his 80s. It's something I noticed in him and something I admire in him, his motivation."

"Jerry doesn't have an agenda. He would write in a balanced way, which doesn't mean that it was a positive way. But he wrote what was there, and he didn't fictionalize and he wrote with balance."
-Ira Berkow

The pantheon of sportswriting greats includes Red Smith and Jerry Izenberg and a fellow named Ira Berkow, who wrote a biography of the former and befriended the latter.

Berkow's "Red: A Biography of Red Smith," was published in 1986. He and Izenberg were established writers at that time, with Berkow working at The New York Times.

A decade younger than Izenberg, Berkow cited his older colleague as a valuable source while looking back at his Red Smith book. Decades later, Berkow pointed out that his impressions of Izenberg were greatly formed from an interview they did for the book.

"Whatever views I have of Jerry came from that interview, really, and how he started and the advice that Red Smith gave him," Berkow recalled.

In the book, Berkow highlighted a defining moment in Izenberg's career: his return to the Newark Star-Ledger in 1962 to become a columnist. From the start, though, his nerves got the best of him. Which is why Red Smith's words of wisdom calmed his nerves.

Berkow described the significance of that advice this way: "When Jerry Izenberg later began writing a column for the Newark Star-Ledger," he spoke to Smith about

it. "Izenberg was having 'a terrible time, everything seemed labored,'" he said. "Red's advice was to 'take a week and try to go to an event every day. If you write off an event, it's much easier. Just make your mind like a big wet piece of clay, and then the event makes an impression on you and that's what you write. You're trying to make it much more complicated than it is.' I was a nervous wreck, and that helped. It helped a lot."

Years later, Izenberg understood his role as a mentor could benefit younger writers.

"I came to New York in 1967 and I started on the book after Red died in 1982," Berkow remembered in an interview. "I had been in New York for 15 years and writing a column and had been in the press boxes and gotten to know Jerry. And he was always a gentleman and always there to give advice or assistance to a young writer. He was someone you knew that you could go to with a question about work and he would be there and be helpful."

Among sportswriters with the gravitas and industry knowledge from the Vietnam War era to the present, Berkow has seen Izenberg's work up close and personal again and again.

This perspective helped Berkow explain why Izenberg mattered greatly to the profession and why his contributions still resonate with those who are really paying attention to quality.

"I've always respected him as a writer and as a person," said Berkow, a reporter and sports columnist for The Times from 1981-2007. "His heart was always in the right place and so was his pen in the days when we used to use pens."

Berkow's association with Izenberg began when he started writing a column for the Newspaper Enterprise Association, a news syndication company. It gave him the chance to deliver commentary on the World Series, heavyweight title fights, Super Bowls, among other marquee events. By being around the major events of the day, Berkow interacted with Jerry and saw how he handled the demands of the job.

"He was always a pleasure to be around and he had a very good social conscience, which I had hoped that I would have, and he was a concerned writer and a robust writer," Berkow said.

"I didn't read the Newark paper a lot, but whenever I had an opportunity to read it Jerry was always displayed prominently and it was always a pleasure to read and informative."

What's more, Red Smith's influence on Izenberg was apparent to Berkow.

"Red Smith was a literary figure in America, not too many sportswriters were, but there were some good sportswriters around. But Red handled the language in an unusual and beautiful way, so he influenced so many of us," stated Berkow, who cited Smith, Jimmy Cannon and Robert Lipsyte as "important influences" while confirming Izenberg belongs in that category, too.

In Berkow's view, Izenberg's work was defined by style and substance.

"He cared about the language and he cared about social issues," Berkow said in 2016.

In other words, what Izenberg wrote mattered a great deal to him.

"Jerry was a concerned citizen who had a platform and he used it and did not abuse it," Berkow commented. "Race relations or gender relations, he was at the forefront of social issues, and I admired that and probably learned from it."

Smith also noticed this. He once called Izenberg "one of the best-informed conscientious writers in sports."

Throughout the years, Berkow observed Izenberg's interactions with sources, seeing him cultivate and maintain relationships with players, coaches, managers, team executives and sports industry officials from across the United States and beyond.

"Jerry had a good personality and there was a sense of a strong character with Jerry that was obvious," Berkow said, "and I think that a source or someone he was interviewing or building a relationship with that besides Jerry having a platform of a column in a major paper there was a sense of strong character that you would respect. That goes a long way toward building a relationship."

Building relationships is one thing, but maintaining relationships can be even harder to accomplish.

But Izenberg voiced his opinions with conviction and maintained friendships for decades with some of the biggest names in sports, including Muhammad Ali and Pete Rozelle.

"Jerry doesn't have an agenda," Berkow insisted. "He would write in a balanced way, which doesn't mean that it was a positive way. But he wrote what was there, and he didn't fictionalize and he wrote with balance.

"Sometimes, if he's going to write negatively about somebody he interviewed, they probably won't like it, but that doesn't mean that it wasn't true. And surely, it would have been true if Jerry wrote it. Or true in his eyes."

After composing his Star-Ledger column for decades, Izenberg's legacy is quite obvious.

Just ask Berkow.

"His legacy is that he was a serious and accomplished journalist," Berkow concluded. "In our business, we've had amateurs and semi-professionals, but Jerry was, as far as I was concerned, an admired professional."

"He was one of the greats of this era, absolutely."
-Dave Anderson

Few sports journalists can claim they have—or had—the same breadth of knowledge about Jerry Izenberg as Dave Anderson.

That statement, composed in June 2018, underscores the longevity of both men's lives, and highlights their contributions to sports journalism, particularly newspapers.

Anderson, born in New York in May 1929, graduated from high school in 1947, the same year that Jackie Robinson of the Brooklyn Dodgers broke Major League Baseball's color barrier. And Anderson was a sharp observer of contemporary sports media and its rich history, which was evident during a phone interview in 2016 for this book. (He passed away in October 2018.)

The retired New York Times sports columnist lamented the decline of general sports columnists in the Internet age, recognizing he and his peers served a valued role in shaping opinions in locales big and small.

"But the way the newspaper business is now, pretty soon there won't be any sports columnists," Anderson said from his New Jersey home.

"Writing on the Internet, writing a blog, isn't the same as a day-to-day newspaper columnist," he added.

Indeed, it's a different era now—and not necessarily a better one.

"All of these blog guys are columnists now, virtually," said Anderson, who won the Pulitzer Prize in 1981, a tribute to his sports commentary. Other sportswriters who have won the Pulitzer include Arthur Daley, Red Smith and Jim Murray.

Added Anderson: "What do they have in their background that made them so readable? And who cares what these guys say? What have they done? Just because it's on the Internet doesn't mean it's worthwhile."

Izenberg, on the other hand, developed a distinct style while crafting memorable prose. His opinions have always been backed by pertinent facts and a keen observer's understanding of how to tell a story.

Anderson, who wrote for the Brooklyn Eagle and New York Journal-American before moving on to The New York Times in 1966, said that Izenberg wrote columns that would jump out at you.

It was, Anderson stated, "just his style."

"To me, it's a Jerry Izenberg style. ... It's like your blood type, only it's words."

With a Red Smith Award on his resume, Izenberg belongs in the "Hall of Fame as a sportswriter in this country," Anderson declared.

Anderson and Izenberg became acquainted with one other in the mid-1950s. Anderson couldn't remember exactly when, but thought it probably was at a New York Giants NFL game in 1956 at Yankee Stadium when they first crossed paths.

Later on, during their extensive coverage of a golden age of heavyweight boxing, they became better acquainted.

In the 1970s, Anderson recalled, he saw Izenberg overseas during a trio of Muhammad Ali fights: The Rumble in the Jungle, Ali vs. George Foreman, in October 1974, in Kinshasa, the Democratic Republic of Congo (now Zaire); Ali vs. Joe Bugner, in July 1975, in Kuala Lumpur; and The Thrilla in Manila, Ali vs. Joe Frazier, in October 1975.

"Those were my favorite, my memorable trips with Jerry," stated Anderson, who was inducted into the National Sportscasters and Sportswriters Hall of Fame in 1990, four years before he received the Red Smith Award.

"When you are covering an event, you are kind of concentrating on yourself," he went on, "so you're not that aware of other people—you're concentrating on the event and what you're trying to think about and write about—but he was great fun to be with whenever we traveled. But he was also a great worker."

Expanding on that point, Anderson noted that "I've always admired the guys, and I was always the same way, that not only did their newspaper work but also magazine articles and books."

Anderson was a prolific reporter and columnist. During his illustrious career, he also wrote more than 20 books and 350 magazine articles.

"But he also went beyond that," Anderson said of Izenberg, citing "Sports Extra," a Sunday evening TV program that aired on Channel 5 in New York City in the 1970s. That program aired for eight years, and remains a memorable distributor of sports tales and opinions for adults of a certain age.

As a pundit, Izenberg crafted commentary that stood the test of time, Anderson insisted, explaining that Izenberg knew what he was doing and had a true passion for the work.

"He was a wonderful writer," Anderson said. "He was a very colorful writer. If you just sit down and somebody gave you five different columns without the bylines from five different writers, you could pick out which one was Jerry Izenberg's because that was his style. He was a very stylistic writer and a very good writer. He had humor in it, but also a lot of serious thoughts, and he also did some great books."

With the conversation shifting to books, Anderson mentioned that he loved Izenberg's "No Medals For Trying: A Week in the Life of a Pro Football Team," about the 1989 New York Giants, who were coached by Bill Parcells. The book focused on Nov. 27-Dec. 3, 1989, with Izenberg giving readers an inside look at the team's day-to-day routines over the course of that week.

"That was one of coach Bill Parcells' favorite phrases: You don't get medals for trying. You've got to win," Anderson said.

Fast forward to 2014, when Izenberg published "Rozelle: A Biography," his authoritative account of the late NFL commissioner Pete Rozelle's life and legacy.

"Even in his so-called retirement now, he did a wonderful book on Pete Rozelle, a lot of which he saved from his notes from interviews with Rozelle, and it showed what a great craftsman and journalist he is," said Anderson.

Asked what is Izenberg's greatest attribute or strength as a journalist, Anderson responded without hesitation: "Devotion to the job."

Because of that devotion, Izenberg earned the rightful reputation as a voice of authenticity about New Jersey. His opinions mattered. His convictions carried weight.

"I think he was the sports conscience of New Jersey," Anderson insisted, "whether it was Rutgers University, whether it was basketball or football there, but he always had, which he should've had, he was writing for a New Jersey newspaper.

"The good and the bad of New Jersey was very important to Jerry."

Did that extend to New York as well?

"To some extent, but he was the only one. I seldom wrote about the conscience of New Jersey, but he did," Anderson said.

***

Izenberg famously developed close ties with Ali. It was a product of the times, according to Anderson.

"There were no barriers with Ali. .... He was always available," Anderson said.

"It was never a barrier, and the main reason for that was (legendary trainer) Angelo Dundee, but again Muhammad Ali went along with it, and there never was a day when Muhammad Ali said 'no comment.' "

Anderson recalled in an interview that he covered 32 of Ali's fights, "probably more than Jerry covered."

Izenberg then confirmed that Anderson was correct, stating that he covered 24 of The Greatest's fights.

While both men enhanced their reputations as sports scribes with distinguished boxing commentary,

Anderson received induction into the International Boxing Hall of Fame in Canastota, New York, in 2008. It took eight more years before Izenberg was given the same accolade.

What took so long?

"I can't answer that. ... He should've been in years ago," Anderson replied.

Nabbing awards, though, has never been Izenberg's main focus. Commitment to his craft and devotion to his community were always at the top of his to-do list.

Anderson cited the Pride Bowl, started in 1979, as a shining example of Izenberg's tireless work on behalf of the community.

In a 2005 feature in the New Jersey Jewish News, writer Ron Kaplan described the decades-long project, for which Izenberg was the president this way: "Project Pride, a Newark-based organization that provides kids with recreational opportunities, after-school tutoring, and college scholarships through proceeds from the annual Pride Bowl football game. The program has raised nearly $4 million and provided almost 1,000 college scholarships since its creation more than 25 years ago."

"I can't think of any other writer (who did this)," Anderson said, "and I'm sure there have been, but certainly not in my recollection locally, that he went out of his way to develop his Pride Bowl, which helped young people in Newark, mostly African-Americans."

"He was the man that got things done," added Anderson.

Sports Illustrated wrote a small article about Project Pride in December 1991.

"People don't understand why I keep doing this," Izenberg told the magazine, "but it's a great feeling to make a difference in the lives of these kids; most of them have no chance."

He got college teams (Seton Hall and Cheyney State competed in the first one; in Pride Bowl XXVIII, Army and Navy squared off in 2005, for example) to play in the game each year, using proceeds from the game to fund computers, science fairs and debate teams, for instance.

"I remember him talking about it almost every time, because I would see him at a lot of Giants football games," Anderson remembered, "and in that era he would always talk to me about it."

People in the business are certainly aware of Izenberg's work, Anderson noted. Then, he said, "Well, I think if he had written for The New York Times or (New York) Daily News or The Washington Post, people would have been much more aware of him.

"The thing that probably is a factor in taking so long to be in the Boxing Hall of Fame is The Star-Ledger just doesn't have the impact that fortunately I had at The Times, that a lot of guys had at various papers. (But) I think that doesn't lessen his worth, let's put it that way."

"He was a thought leader in the world of sports journalism."
-Jeremy Schaap

For nearly his entire life, Jeremy Schaap has been aware of Jerry Izenberg's career. It goes with the territory.

"Obviously my dad knew a lot of the same people," Schaap acknowledged in 2016.

He followed his famous father Dick's footsteps into sports broadcasting, which over the years has given him an insider's look at what makes Jerry tick.

The elder Schaap, a legendary newspaper/magazine reporter, columnist and editor, author and TV broadcaster, died in December 2001. Since his passing, Jeremy has continued to establish himself as one of the most thoughtful and resourceful journalists under the ESPN umbrella.

Schaap was asked to look back on his awareness of Izenberg's career before his own rise to prominence in the business. In doing so, he also took time to reflect on Izenberg's place within the pantheon of prominent sportswriters.

"I didn't grow up reading him on a daily basis," Schaap admitted in a phone interview.

"But I knew his work and then I had the opportunity to work with him side by side for a few years as we did this show called 'Classic Sports Reporters' (on ESPN Classic) and we got to spend a lot of time together and it was a privilege in working with Jerry at that time, which was about 15, 16 years ago, late '90s, early 2000s.

"I came to understand the significance of his work, and Jerry is one of those rare guys who is both a terrific writer and a helluva reporter ... and they are not mutually exclusive, but one doesn't necessarily follow the other."

So what makes Izenberg a significant figure in sports media?

"I think Jerry's important in a lot of ways, but the most important thing about Jerry is that before it was popular to be for most of the sportswriting community had reconsidered its retrograde or reactionary opinions of things Jerry was kind of a trailblazer," stated Schaap, who has written "Cinderella Man: James J. Braddock, Max Baer, and the Greatest Upset in Boxing History" and "Triumph: The Untold Story of Jesse Owens and Hitler's Olympics."

"Well, when I think of Jerry," Schaap added, "I think of the way he championed blacks in baseball who did not get the opportunities that whites got, in particular his close friend Larry Doby."

Schaap recognized that Izenberg remained a persistent voice calling out for racial and social justice for decades. Clearly, that impressed him.

"The dearth of black managers was one of the things, I think, that Jerry wrote about, the mistreatment of the black athlete," Schaap said. "And he was someone who perceived these things, which now seem obvious, before most of his fellow sportswriters did.

"It's a different world now. A lot of sportswriters now are guys with liberal arts degrees and they come at things from a more left-of-center orientation. It wasn't that way generations ago. It was more of a trade and there were fewer guys who were socially aware, racially aware, and Jerry was really in the vanguard, and I think that's to his eternal credit."

Dick Schaap edited Sport magazine in the 1970s, seeking out distinguished writers and original voices to fill its pages, including Izenberg.

The NYC-based magazine, which printed its final issue in 2000, was impressive in its heyday, according to Izenberg.

"In its glory years, the magazine had great editors who gave writers freedom and a forum to say things that mattered," Izenberg was quoted as saying in "Thomas Hauser on Sports: Remembering the Journey."

"It was an authentic voice that brought out the best in us," Izenberg said of Sport.

For Jeremy Schaap, that quality resonates to this day.

"Jerry Izenberg was one of those names growing up in the sportswriting business where I always knew Jerry's name," Jeremy pointed out. "I'm sure I saw his name in the best sportswriting anthologies and in Sport and around. ... Izenberg was one of the big guys, and I can't pinpoint where I first heard of him, but I can't really imagine a time when I didn't know who Jerry was."

***

It's no secret why Izenberg has thrived as a columnist in the cut-throat New York metropolitan media market for decades.

In short, he's a gifted communicator.

"When I think of Jerry I think of somebody who had a way of communicating with athletes so that he got good stuff," Schaap said. "These were reported columns. They were reported, they were written.

"When I think of Jerry's columns, I think of a guy who went out and did the hard work of column writing. He wasn't sitting there on Sunday afternoon or Saturday night, thinking, like, 'Jeez, what the hell am I gonna write about this week?', because he had done the work, he had the contacts. His entire life had been building relationships, establishing a viewpoint, and that kind of rich column that is hued with historical perspective, with the actual effort, shoe-leather effort of going out and getting it, and more than anything else a guy who isn't a cheap-shot artist, who isn't a sensationalist, is someone with a point of

view, but it's all girded by a sense of humanity.

"That's what I think of when I think of Jerry is somebody who's interested in being fair, and also interested in taking a strong opinion, but not for the sake of taking a strong opinion or expressing one.

"He takes his work very seriously, he takes the world of sports very seriously, and he understands th impact that sports can have on society at large, and that's the space that he occupied."

Perhaps more than most Schaap understands that Izenberg always saw the big picture: that sports aren't just games, but a microcosm of society.

"A lot of guys kind of bemoan the fact like, 'Uh, I just want to write about the games. I don't want to deal with all the social issues and all of that stuff, '" Schaap commented. "Jerry thrives and pries at the intersection of society and sports."

***

When Muhammad Ali died in June 2016, the massive file of columns and broadcast archives that occupied Izenberg's time over the decades entered a new place. It became a primary source of Ali's life and times.

It also helped remind anyone who wasn't paying attention how vital Izenberg had been in chronicling The Greatest's career and much, much more.

"People in the business know Jerry," Schaap said. "People who have an appreciation for history as sportswriting know that Jerry is a big figure in a big market. "

As they had done at many marquee sports events of the past few decades, Schaap and Izenberg crossed paths in Las Vegas in September 2015 for the Floyd Mayweather Jr.-Andre Berto welterweight world title fight at MGM Grand Garden Arena. The fight, won by Mayweather, provided a recent opportunity for Schaap to observe Izenberg at the top of his game.

"He loves the work. He loves the writing," Schaap noted. "And to be writing columns for as long as he has, that's amazing. It's remarkable and there's passion for it."

Earlier in Schaap's career, before he became a prominent figure at ESPN and not merely a young up-and-comer with a famous dad, he witnessed the passion that Izenberg brought to every aspect of his work.

Boxing brought that trait under the big spotlight.

"I was always surprised when we did that show 'Classic Sports Reporters' together how passionately Jerry felt about things (and these) guys," Schaap recalled. "We'd get into arguments about, like, Ezzard Charles or Joe Walcott vs. Rocky Marciano, and I was like, 'Jerry, the fight was 50 years ago. Let it go.' But he still feels things deeply, and that's the thing, that kind of enthusiasm is very hard to manufacture. It's either there or it isn't—that kind of passion for what you're doing.

"Most guys by the time they reach their early 70s, or late 60s when I was working with Jerry, that enthusiasm has dissipated and they've mellowed. And I would say Jerry's enthusiasm has not dissipated and he has not mellowed."

Ali's close friendship with Izenberg, which lasted for most of the boxer's life, demonstrated again that the latter was truly unique. And to his credit, it showed that Jerry valued Muhammad as a human being and not just as a famous source to fill space in his column, even when Ali was criticized profusely by many for changing his name from Cassius Clay, embracing the Black Muslim faith and for refusing to serve in the U.S. military during the Vietnam War.

"I think when it comes to Ali is that there were Ali champions, there were Ali detractors. Izenberg was somebody again, like he had been on many issues, ahead of the curve," Schaap said. "And at the time, he might have seemed like an outlier, but eventually history would vindicate him."

There are parallels in any timeline that charts Howard Cosell's support for Ali and Izenberg's. The broadcasting giant, of course, had the bigger forum—and the bombastic personality as well. But that didn't diminish Izenberg's moral crusade; in fact, it might've kept him more focused in shedding light on the issue with razor-sharp commentary.

"It's hard to make the same kind of impact writing a column as you do when you've got that platform of network television, but I would say that Jerry was on the right side of history again as he was so often," Schaap said.

"...Certainly it was good for Ali to have champions in the press, to have champions in the white media, but he's still Muhammad Ali without Howard, and I think he's still Muhammad Ali without Jerry. But the support was not irrelevant."

In 2016, Izenberg appeared on Schaap's ESPN Radio program, "A Sporting Life," prior to Super Bowl 50. And it was a big reminder of the depth of Jerry's sporting knowledge and the history connected to the personalities, games, teams and leagues that he's written about for decades.

"It's always a win having Jerry on because there's so much perspective, there's so much energy," Schaap said. "I hope when I'm 86 that I have an iota of the passion and the energy and the creativity that Jerry still has. He's a witness to really the entire second half of the 20th century in sports and of the beginning of the 21st, and he opens this witness for us unto a time when things were very different in many respects and so it's always fun hearing what he has to say."

***

I asked Schaap to state what's the greatest compliment he can make about Izenberg's career. His answer provided nuance and insight beyond the typical sound bite heard during contemporary political campaigns.

"I would say the best thing you can say about Jerry also happens to be true: that he made an impact," Schaap said. "He made an impact because he didn't follow, but he led. He was a thought leader in the world of sports journalism, and it's easy to be part of the pack. It's easy to pile on, and that wasn't Jerry.

He went on: "Jerry is a fiercely independent thinker and a gifted writer and somebody with a heart and I think all those things that he was able to make an impact in a way that even more prominent writers might not have, because he was concerned with social issues, he was concerned with racial justice issues. He wasn't the kind of guy despite his age, despite the circumstances of his own life, was going to condemn a (Tommie) Smith and a (John) Carlos as so many did.

"He was somebody because of the circumstances of his own life who also understood the issues facing America, and he was part of that generation, as my father was, who grappled with and wrote about and I think came to understand the significance of the black athlete," Schaap concluded.

"I have published dozens of sports books over the years, many of them quite successful, but no one has ever come close to what Jerry accomplished."
-Rick Wolff

Legendary announcer Bob Wolff passed away in July 2017 at age 96, several months after he and his son, Rick, took part in an email interview for this book.

At the time of the interview, the elder Wolff was 95 and held the distinction of being the world's longest-running sportscaster, according to Guinness World Records. His career began in 1938 and he remained on the air at Cablevision Long Island until his final days. He was honored by both the National Baseball Hall of Fame and Naismith Memorial Basketball Hall of Fame for his broadcasting career.

Rick relayed these anecdotes after conversing with his father about Jerry: "Their paths crossed for years when dad was broadcasting the Knicks and Rangers at MSG (Madison Square Garden), and dad told me: 'Jerry was always a delight to talk with, because he was sharp, did his homework, and had terrific insights. Plus he has a great sense of humor.' "

For a few years, Bob Wolff oversaw a sportscasting and sportswriting class at Seton Hall University, where Jerry "was always a mainstay lecturer," Rick stated.

Bob recalled, "My wife Jane and I would go out to dinner with Jerry after the classes, and he was charming, well-versed, and a lot of fun. We traded lots of stories about the sports media, our colleagues, and so on. In short, I really enjoyed Jerry's company. A real good guy and, as a writer, a real pro."

Rick Wolff, senior executive editor at Houghton Mifflin Harcourt in New York, recalled a memorable chapter in his own career that involved books, sports and Izenberg.

"Sometime in the early fall of 1989, I received a phone call from Jay Action, who at the time was a well-known literary agent who specialized in sports books," Wolff recalled.

"Jay told me that Jerry Izenberg, the famed sports columnist, had somehow gotten clearance from Bill Parcells and the New York Giants to sit in every one of their daily meetings during the week leading up to a crucial game against the Philadelphia Eagles.

"This, of course, was unheard of. Parcells was at his peak, and his star players were Lawrence Taylor and Phil Simms. I remember saying to Jay, 'There's no way in the world that Parcells would ever let anyone sit in his private team meetings - and especially not Jerry Izenberg!' "

It wasn't fake news, as Rick quickly found out.

"But Jay was adamant. So I spoke with Jerry, and asked him about this amazing access to the Giants," Wolff said. "He told me that he couldn't tell me how he had arranged this, but he absolutely assured me that it was a done deal. Convinced, we did a publishing deal, and Jerry went to work. Starting with the team's flight back to New York from a grueling loss to San Francisco on Nov. 28, 1989, and for the next six days and nights, Izenberg maintained an extensive diary of every key team meeting, coaching session and behind-the-scenes conversations with the Giants' players, trainers and coaches. They were totally focused on trying to come up with a game plan to stop the Eagles multi-talented quarterback, Randall Cunningham. Days started well before dawn, and lasted until midnight. The only constant was Jerry's presence.

"Jerry wrote an entire book from his taking notes from those meetings. In fact, there really aren't any chapters in the book; rather, there are just day and time stamps, as in: Tuesday, 10 AM, Bill Parcells'office, or Thursday, 4 PM, Trainers' Room.

"Along the way, you got a real sense of how many long, long hours these coaches and their players put into preparing for that next game. You got to know them not just as Sunday warriors, but as real people with real worries, real injuries and real pain. Plus the gnawing insecurity of life in the National Football League, not to mention having a bear of a head coach like Parcells breathing down your neck."

The exhaustive effort paid off in a big way.

"In the end, the book was simply magnificent," Wolff declared. "Entitled 'NO MEDALS FOR TRYING: A Week in the Life of a Pro Football Team,' the book was a smash success," said Wolff. "No one had ever attempted to do this kind of in-the-trenches reporting before, because quite frankly, no professional team or coaching staff would ever dream of allowing a veteran sportswriter like Jerry Izenberg this kind of access.

"But Jerry somehow pulled it off, and the book is considered a classic. By the way, NO MEDALS FOR TRYING is from Bill Parcells, who would warn his Giants that you have no choice except to win ...'because there are no medals for trying in this league.' "

In the end, Izenberg's work became an unforgettable, glorious chapter in Wolff's career as an editor.

"I have published dozens of sports books over the years, many of them quite successful, but no one has ever come close to what Jerry accomplished," Wolff concluded. "To this day, I feel honored and privileged to have watched him make this magic happen."

"He didn't use a velvet sieve like Red Smith, but he didn't peel a grape with an ax, either. He was somewhere in between the two."

-John Schulian

Jerry Izenberg has produced important journalism during multiple eras, working with reporters and editors who returned to the United States as World War II military veterans and chasing deadlines alongside men and women who came of age in the post-9/11 era.

Longevity is one thing.

Sustained relevance is another.

Izenberg hasn't remained relevant just because of his age. He has a timeless gift for storytelling.

John Schulian, a prominent observer of Jerry's career and one of the most distinguished sports columnists of the past half century, can properly assess Izenberg's place in the pantheon of ink-stained newspaper scribes.

Schulian has retired from the daily grind of pounding out a column, which he did with verve for The Washington Post, Chicago Sun-Times, Chicago Daily News and Philadelphia Daily News before a switch to TV writing and producing. In 1986, he joined the "Miami Vice" staff as a writer and later made his mark as co-creator of "Xena: Warrior Princess."

But Schulian has kept a close eye on sports journalism, following the work of his peers and the overall industry. In 2014, he edited "Football: Great Writing About the National Sport," a Library of America anthology. In recent years, he also conceptualized and edited Library of America's "The Great American Sports Page: A Century of Classic Columns from Ring Lardner to Sally Jenkins" and along with his late co-editor George Kimball assembled its "At the Fights: American Writers on Boxing" anthology.

Izenberg's work has always impressed him.

He noted that Izenberg "wrote during the Golden Age of sportswriting and now sportswriting is whatever it's become, which certainly isn't what it was 20, 25, 30, 40, even 50 years ago."

In Schulian's opinion, "Jerry was a terrific writer and he had a social conscience and broke a lot of new ground. Whether he was writing about Eddie Robinson down at Grambling or the emergence of the National Football League or big fights, he was there at a lot of epic events."

Now in his 70s, Schulian can recall stumbling upon Izenberg's work in one of E.P. Dutton's "Best Sports Series" anthologies, a 1944-80 project spearheaded by a New York Herald Tribune assistant sports editor, Irving T. Marsh, and a high school English teacher, Edward Ehre.

"That's where I read Jerry first," noted Schulian, who attended high school and college in Salt Lake City, Utah.

"(And) you didn't have a lot of great sports writing locally," he added. "It was pretty slim pickings, so you read Sports Illustrated, which was emerging as a powerhouse, and then you got out-of-town papers in the journalism department at the University of Utah, where I went to school, and then you were left to your own devices. And when I read the Best Sports Stories there were rows of them ... and I'd see stories that caught my eye for the way they were written. I was probably more interested in how they were written than what they were written about.

"Probably the first thing I ever read by Jerry was a piece he wrote about a World Series game, maybe the Yankees and Dodgers from '63."

Life marched on. Schulian attended grad school at Northwestern University in Illinois and served in the U.S. Army for a few years.

In 1970, he traveled to New York for the first time.

"I had a job interview at Sports Illustrated and one at Merrill Lynch because my old journalism professor crossed over and was trying to work for the Evil Empire and wanted me to become a public relations man with him, which I was extremely unsuited for," he admitted with a laugh.

During that trip to the Big Apple, Schulian was reintroduced to Izenberg's work.

"I picked up a copy of Jock Magazine, and here was a story by Jerry Izenberg about how they used race to promote these wrestling matches at Madison Square Garden," Schulian recalled. "You know, you'd have the blond guy against the black guy, the Puerto Rican guy against the white guy, or the Puerto Rican guy against the black guy. It was fascinating stuff because Jerry was looking at sports or quasi-sports, I guess in the case of professional wrestling, seriously, even though the stories were colorful and lively. But he was saying, Look, somebody's promoting or taking advantage of the racial strife, if you will, or racial conflict to make a buck in the name of sports. So it was interesting stuff."

"That showed Jerry to be a thoughtful guy, a guy who thought about a lot of stuff. And then somewhere down the line, to go back to the Best Sports Stories anthology, I read his great piece on Grambling, which had run in True magazine."

The piece he referenced was Izenberg's September 1967 groundbreaking feature on Robinson's college football team. Schulian selected that story for inclusion in the aforementioned Football anthology.

The article was a landmark piece of print journalism. The story expanded its reach with the production of "Grambling: 100 Yards of Glory," a 1968 documentary that aired on WABC TV in New York in a less-than-ideal time slot for mass exposure (Saturday, 10:30 p.m.; Howard Cosell was the executive producer).

Six months after its debut in New York, the documentary aired on prime time and was nominated for an Emmy award. Izenberg wrote and directed the documentary.

Looking back on the two projects, Schulian mentioned that Izenberg's characteristics as a journalist shone through.

"Jerry was a hustler," he said. "Jerry had many virtues."

***

Schulian said he can't pinpoint a precise time and place where he first crossed paths with Izenberg.

"Sportswriters are interesting. A lot of times we don't get formal introductions because we know each other's work before we know the guy, and you read somebody and you say, 'I might like Jerry Izenberg or I might like Red Smith.' And the next thing you know you are sitting in the press box next to them, and you just sort of start chatting and that's how friendships begin," he said.

"I don't ever remember somebody saying, 'John, this is Jerry Izenberg, or Jerry, this is John Schulian.' We just knew each other."

And they met sometime in the mid-1970s, according to Schulian.

What was Jerry like in those days?

"He was lively and he was full of opinions and he was great fun to be around," Schulian said.

Izenberg's experiences in the business and working knowledge of New York sports media were invaluable to Schulian when he penned the introduction for a reissued journalism classic, Stanley Woodward's "Paper Tiger: An Old Sportswriter's Reminiscences of People, Newspapers, War, and Work." The University of Nebraska Press published the book in April 2007.

Schulian first spoke to Izenberg when he was preparing the introduction.

"Jerry worked for Stanley Woodward. That in and of itself qualifies him as a museum piece," Schulian said of Woodward, who died in 1964.

Woodward was "one of the great sports editors of all time, maybe the greatest sports editor of all time," Schulian declared, "and Jerry took his lead from Stanely Woodward. He pointed him in the right direction, gave him good advice and didn't let him be a young knucklehead, either."

That advice influenced Izenberg a great deal, as he's mentioned on many occasions.

***

So what are the trademarks of Izenberg's writing style? What immediately stands out?

"With Jerry, you always get a certain ferocity," Schulian observed. "I think he's pugnacious, but I don't mean it in a Dick Young way. I just mean that he's lively. He's full of opinions, and you get a sense that he's been there, that he knows whereof what he writes. He got close to a lot of important people in sports—Pete Rozelle, Larry Holmes, (Muhammad) Ali. He was probably as close to a lot of his subjects as a sportswriter can be.

"It's hard enough work doing the job properly, but to maintain friendships or alliances or just good professional relationships can be difficult because a lot of times what you write in the paper is not necessarily what ballplayers or team owners or coaches or managers want to read. And Jerry was able to be tough and have real standards and yet he didn't turn these guys off for life."

Schulian then delivered one of the best lines that have ever been expressed about Izenberg.

"He didn't use a velvet sieve like Red Smith, but he didn't peel a grape with an ax, either. He was somewhere in between the two," Schulian offered.

Izenberg also understood how to get unique, original content. He relied on instincts and common sense.

"I think a lot of his best work was probably done away from the pack," Schulian added.

"And I don't think you get a lot of views if you're always hanging in the crowd and listening to people. I think Jerry was a guy who would grab Angelo Dundee and say, 'Ang, do you have a minute? Can we go somewhere private and talk?' I get the feeling that that's the way Jerry worked, because that's what I would try to do.

"Sometimes you have very specific questions that you want to ask, and you don't want the whole world to hear them, because you are looking for stuff that concerns you, or that interests you, and that you think will interest your readers."

***

In any interview about Izenberg, his longevity in the newspaper biz is a worthwhile topic.

Asking about his top attributes as a writer and pundit also elicits interesting responses.

To wit: What's the greatest compliment you can make about his career and body of work?

"There's so much to admire about Jerry," Schulian stated. " I mean, look at him now: He's long past retirement age, and there's no quit in the man. He's always speaking of the next story, the next book, the next hurdle, the next mountain to climb.

"And that to me really says a lot about him, that he's still vibrant, that he's still interested in these things ... interested in writing about them and sharing what he's learned and what he's seen, and he's seen so much. So I really, really just think the world of him for that—that he's intrepid.

"When I look at my life now that I'm officially a senior citizen, that's how I want to spend my golden years. I don't want to just watch the rest of the world go by. I mean, there are days when I don't mind doing that, but I always like to have something cooking, some project that I'm working on, and to see a guy like Jerry doing it is inspiring to me."

Schulian didn't stop there. He had ample praise for Izenberg's work ethic and progressive mindset on the job.

"When you speak of his body of work as a whole, you just have to acknowledge him as one of the real progressive sportswriters of the 20th century," Schulian added. "That he was a guy who didn't get as much attention for it as, say, Robert Lipsyte or Larry Merchant or people like that, and those guys were great sportswriters. But Jerry worked the same turf they did, and he was just as progressive in his way as they were in theirs—that he was breaking new ground, that he wasn't falling back on cliches, that he was fearless. He was going after things. He was daring to be different. He didn't mind swimming against the tide.

"There was that pugnaciousness, I think, that he possessed that really served him well in that era."

"He would often tell you a story within the story."
-Wallace Matthews

Decades before the ubiquitous presence of game highlights on 24-hour cable sports networks, there was a wise, distinguished pundit named Jerry Izenberg delivering thoughtful commentary on a Sunday night TV program in Gotham.

He was a unique voice in New York-area sports then. And now, he's still pounding away on the keyboard, even though he's not on TV as often these days.

Wallace Matthews recognizes how impressive Izenberg's career has been. Just ask him. You won't—you can't—get a 20-second summary of his admiration for Jerry.

So pull up a seat, relax and get ready for the full story...

One of the premier voices in NYC sports journalism over the past few decades, Matthews has developed a large following during stops at the New York Post and Newsday and ESPN. He's written for The New York Times, Forbes.com, and Yahoo Sports and elsewhere in recent years.

He considers Izenberg an important mentor, a key role model and a dear friend.

To support his friend, Matthews attended Izenberg's book-signing event for "Once There Were Giants: The Golden Age of Heavyweight Boxing" at Barnes and Noble in Staten Island, New York, in mid-March 2017.

It was an appropriate gesture.

Matthews' ties to Izenberg connect his youth to his longtime profession. That link is sports.

For most of life, the native New Yorker has paid attention to Izenberg's work, starting out with what he said on TV.

"I became aware of him back in the '70s when he was doing the TV show called 'Sports Extra,' on Channel 5 (WNEW) here, FOX in New York," Matthews said in an interview. "Versatile Bill Mazer cohosted the program as part of his 20-year run at the station."

Matthews called the show "a forerunner of the sports wrap-up show."

In the early-to-mid-1970s, while in high school, Matthews recalled, "it was the last thing I'd watch before I go to bed, because the next day would be a school day, and it was the forerunner of (ESPN's) 'SportsCenter.' ... It basically wrapped up the whole week because it was on Sunday. ... And at the very end they bring on this guy who comes on and does like an on-camera essay, and it was Jerry.

"And I loved him because he was just a different-looking guy. He had a goatee back then when nobody had one. To me, he was like a jazz musician or something. His wire-rimmed glasses, he had the goatee, and he talked in this gruff New York voice, and it sounded like a guy who didn't take any shit from anybody. And I used to look forward to the end; that was to me the highlight of the show, when Jerry would come on.

"I used to always look forward to him talking about boxing, because I was a big boxing fan. That was my thing."

Matthews recalled boxing, football and horse racing were staples of Jerry's "Sports Extra" essays.

"The best memories I'll have of becoming a journalist, and I've told this to my kids, is that, it's funny, the people that you admire as a kid somehow become your colleagues and your friends," Matthews said. "I couldn't believe that later on I became friends with Jerry Izenberg. I used to watch this guy on TV.

"He's been a cherished friend. We've been together on a lot of events and two in particular, one because of a personal incident."

He continued: "We were at the Belmont Stakes and I guess this was in the '90s and the horse was going for the Triple Crown, either Silver Charm or Real Quiet, in 1998 or '99, I think, because my son had just been born and he was like a year-and-a-half old and Jerry insisted that he had to buy my newborn son a Tshirt, a Belmont Stakes T-shirt and we still have that 20 years later. That was such a cool thing."

Matthews graduated from high school in 1975.

So when did he first meet his newspaper idol?

He pinpointed the Marvin Hagler-Thomas Hearns middleweight title fight on April 15, 1985, at Caesars Palace, "because that was the first major fight that I did in Las Vegas and all the guys were there, all the major boxing writers were there."

Matthews became part of that fraternity by being around the action, inside and outside the ring, including the Larry Holmes-Michael Spinks heavyweight title bout in 1985.

"I knew Jerry because we were part of a group that walked out on Larry Holmes when he had Dick Young thrown out of a workout just before the fight," Matthews said. "And Jerry was one of them."

Asked about when he recognized Jerry's talents as a writer and if that came later than when he saw him on TV, Matthews offered this insight: "I was aware of his work. It's not by accident that I'm in this business. I always read, I devoured the sports (pages) every single day. My family, we had the Daily News delivered to the door in the morning and my dad would come home at the end of the day with the Post under his arm. So I read everything, and Jerry's stuff (his syndicated column) used to appear in the New York Post.

"I was aware of how good he was for a long time. ... I'd read him, I'd read Dick Young. I didn't read the guys who focused on the NBA or baseball. I wasn't as into that. I was into boxing, so he was somebody that I always sought out, and guys like Stan Hochman (of the Philadelphia Daily News)."

What trademarks characterized his writing?

"I thought he was more literary than most of them," Matthews said. "He would often tell you a story within the story, and he does that in conversation, too. If he wants to tell you a story about Muhammad Ali, he'll start by telling you about the fight between Cain and Abel or something like that.

"He'll give you the perspective of why it matters, why this parallels to (something else). I always liked that about him, plus I always had the sense that he was a bit of a wise ass and I found out later that he is.

"That came through in his writing, as I said before, he's the type that didn't take any shit from anybody. To me, he was like the quintessential New York wise guy .... and that's what I wanted to be."

***

It shouldn't be very surprising that Jerry Izenberg and New York Yankees icon Yogi Berra developed—and maintained—a close bond over the years.

"Jerry and Yogi were very close," Matthews shared.

Berra, of course, represented winning as a clutch player on the 1940s-60s Yankee dynasty (14 World Series appearances, 10 title-winning teams), while later serving as a pennant-winning manager for both the Yankees and Mets.

And then when Yankees principal owner George Steinbrenner fired him 16 games into the 1985 season, breaking his promise to Yogi, their feud reached epic proportions. Yogi didn't set foot in Yankee Stadium for an official event for 14 years.

"Yogi said I'm never going back," Matthews remembered.

Their epic feud ended in January 1999, when Steinbrenner visited the all-time great at the Yogi Berra Museum in Montclair, New Jersey, and apologized.

And here's where Matthews picked up the story. "They've had their reconciliation and it's the day before he's going to come back to Yankee Stadium. ... It was Old Timer's Day or something and Yogi was going to make his return to Yankee Stadium, and I was talking to Jerry in the Yankee clubhouse.

"He looks at me with a strange face and says, 'This is what you write. Yogi's a schmuck. He should never come back. He should tell George Steinbrenner to go fuck himself.'

"So I said, 'You know what, Jerry, that's not bad.'

"I just fuckin' killed Yogi for giving in (to) George. And the next day I saw Jerry and he said, 'Yogi's going to kill you.'

"What do you mean?"

"He's really pissed off about that column.

"I said, 'You told me to write it!

"I didn't think you were really going to write it, you schmuck."

Looking back, "that was a lesson learned, right?" Matthews offered with a laugh. ("It actually wasn't a bad column, but yes, Yogi was pissed off.")

"I must say this: That Jerry presented the column that that's what he was going to write. So the next day when I said to him, 'But you told me this was the column,' he said, 'I wasn't going to write that. What are you crazy?'

"He basically played me."

And Matthews' infamous column became a running conversation between Wallace and Jerry.

"Until Yogi died, Jerry would always say to me, 'Yogi's looking for you,' " Matthews said. "And to me that's kind of Jerry's personality in a nutshell right there."

***

Legacy is a theme that writers like to ponder from time to time, and gathering viewpoints about Izenberg's legacy is far from boring.

Matthews weighed in, too.

"I think that first of all he's one of the few guys in this business that's universally respected," Matthews said. "I've never heard anybody question his integrity or question his intentions.

"Anybody that's been able to cover 50 Super Bowls and still get along with the players, the owners and the commissioner is pretty remarkable.

"The other thing is just look at the sheer number of halls of fame that he's been voted into between the New Jersey Hall of Fame, the International Jewish Sports Hall of Fame, the International Boxing Hall of Fame, I think that obviously says a lot to what his legacy is and how respected he is. And it's not just a longevity thing. ... It's not that because Jerry had this reputation when I first met him 30 years ago, so it's not like he needed to hang around to be 86 years old to get this.

"He was respected back then. I think he was always considered to be fair. You have to remember how ahead of his time this guy was. I mean you're talking about a white man, a white Jewish man from New York in the '60s supporting Muhammad Ali, supporting Cassius Clay/Muhammad Ali."

And then Wallace Matthews, who's never shy about expressing his opinion, gave a genuinely Matthews-esque opinion.

"I realize that Howard Cosell gets all the credit for being Ali's (ally), but fuck Howard Cosell. Jerry Izenberg was ahead of that. Howard Cosell did it for ratings," Matthews commented. "He realized this guy was great television, but Jerry realized right from wrong. He didn't see color. He didn't see the phony patriotism of the Vietnam War era. He saw what was right and what was wrong, and that's why Ali respected him. They were friends. They were beyond reporter and subject."

Returning to the aforementioned event at the Barnes and Noble, Matthews tossed out a question during the gathering: "I said, Jerry, what would you pick out as your favorite column that you ever wrote?"

"He said, 'That's a really good question."

Izenberg paused to reflect for a few minutes.

Said Matthews, continuing the story, "He goes, 'I'll tell you something,' and his voice begins to crack, and he actually becomes emotional. And he says, 'I won't say it's my favorite column, but the one I want to be remembered for was my Muhammad Ali obit, because it was really emotional to me, they told me write as long as I want.' "

That column on the global icon was more than 3,100 words. And in an age where tweets are often valued more than quality prose, Izenberg's old-fashioned work was trending on Twitter.

Izenberg's tough-guy persona couldn't hide the pain of Ali's death.

Said Matthews: "It was obvious that it was painful for him to write, that it was something that he didn't want to write. But he was happy with how it came out. I really thought he was going to cry and I've never seen him emotional before."

***

Despite the ultra-competitive media market of New York City and the surrounding suburbs, Matthews said Izenberg earned the respect of his peers, but the competition to have The Story—to outdo Jerry—wasn't really there.

"You were never competing with Jerry. You were waiting to see what Jerry wrote, because you knew he was going to kick your ass," Matthews said, laughing, "whatever it was. But it wasn't like, 'I've got to match Jerry.' "

Instead, he said, "the hope was, what can I learn from Jerry? What did I miss here that he's going to have, and that maybe next time I'll remember to do something like that."

Perhaps Matthews paid the ultimate compliment to Izenberg when he revealed that he remains an avid reader of Jerry's work.

"To this day, and I've been reading him for 40 years, he still has the ability to teach me something," Matthews said. "He still has the ability to impress me. I can read him and where there'll be a turn of phrase there, I'll say, shit, I wish I'd come up with that. To me, that's the biggest compliment because I've been doing this a long time. I'm not the new kid on the block anymore; I'm one of the older guys now.

"But to this day, I'll still read Jerry and he'll show me something. When you get to a certain point, man and you can't be shown anything anymore, you're pretty much done, but he can still show me."

***

Being around boxing for decades, Matthews has met countless tough guys, plenty of phonies and wannabe pugilists as well. But you can't accuse Izenberg of being fake. In essence, he has a distinguished personality that takes a bit of time to unravel.

"If it weren't for the gruff exterior, he's really a warm guy," Matthews said. "He's kind of almost grandfatherly in a way, and he always was. I always felt that way about him way back when, even when he's smacking you because you wrote something or thought something or said something that wasn't quite right, he's doing it in a way to make you better, not to knock you down."

He went on: "I always felt like his criticisms were designed to make you better."

Matthews pointed out that criticism from newspaper editors and colleagues over the years could be summed up this way: "We're not looking to make you better, we're looking to make you feel worse."

To his credit, Izenberg took a different tact.

"He would never be that way," Matthews said of certain editors. "There's a humanity about him, which I think comes through in his writing. You just can't hide that. It's a quality that comes through."

***

When Matthews was asked if he were assigned to write an in-depth magazine profile of Izenberg, what would be the first thing he'd ask him, the younger journalist provided a curiosity-driven answer.

"How did he formulate his world view?" was the way Matthews responded.

But he didn't stop there, of course.

"This is a guy liberal at a time when it wasn't fashionable, racially conscious at a time when most people weren't, who was literary in an era when sportswriting was getting away from that," Matthews added.

"Things were getting more colloquial and he always kept it at a higher level."

In the spring of 2017, Matthews shared a story that Izenberg told about him and his father and growing up in Newark, New Jersey.

Matthews said, "He said that somebody had written on the sidewalk in front of his house in Newark 'no kites allowed.' He said to his dad, 'What does that mean?'

"And his father said, 'First of all, it's not kites. It was kikes. He was saying something (derogatory) about Jews. And if anybody says this word to you, you are supposed to punch him in the mouth, and if you don't finish with the left hook, don't come home.' "

Matthews' reaction to that story from decades ago?

"To me, that's like both sides of Jerry," he said. "There was an extreme toughness about him, but at the same time he was able to view people compassionately. That's a pretty rare quality. A lot of times people are one way or the other, and he's both."

***

Thinking back to the first Mike Tyson-Evander Holyfield heavyweight fight, held in Nevada in November 1996, Matthews recalled a memorable exchange with Izenberg, who sat next to him.

"And we both loved Evander," Matthews said of the huge underdog.

"How am I ever going to be able to teach my kid right from wrong if the rapist beats this guy?" Matthews recalled thinking. "And I think he's really going to hurt him and Jerry felt the same way.

"The fight started and Holyfield just kicked the crap out of him in the first round, and I turned to Jerry and we both just looked at each other and we started to laugh. And I said, 'Jerry, he's getting knocked down tonight.' And he said, 'You're right,' and of course he did."

Holyfield triumphed with an 11-round TKO.

And what was Izenberg's inscription to Matthews for his copy of "Once They Were Giants?"

"To Wally Matthews, who sat next to me at the Tyson fight and saw into the future."

"So he remembered that from 20 years ago," Matthews said.

***

From the days of Sugar Ray Robinson to Sugar Ray Leonard and beyond, Jerry Izenberg has been a gifted chronicler of the sweet science, even though he's distinguished himself as a columnist who can write about anything and do it well.

"Boxing, I think, is where he shines because he can really get into the humanity of the characters involved," Matthews declared.

"You could watch a thousand football games, you don't give a rat's ass who wins. I don't care if Tom Brady throws 12 touchdowns or 12 interceptions, there's no emotional connection.

"But when you cover a fight, you do get to know them as human beings, you also know that what they do is also rooted so deeply in humiliation and pain and sometimes even death. There's so much more at stake.

"If you lose a football game or baseball game, big deal. You come back and play again tomorrow, and you still get paid. That doesn't happen in boxing. Jerry's always been able to bring that out, and I don't think a lot of boxing writers do. I think a lot of them just look at it as jabs and hooks and they don't get to see beyond that.

"Jerry's always been able to communicate that and that's what I try to communicate. So to me there's no comparison, that's where he excels."

Above all, stellar communication skills, empathy and a real interest in people carried Izenberg to the top in his profession. And he's been there for decades, spanning generations of sports fans and journalists. Or put another way: Long before a man set foot on the moon, Izenberg had figured out how to write compelling columns and articles that resonated with readers, stories that were both timeless and timely. Witty and thought-provoking.

An appreciation for history—boxing history, for instance—is a big part of what's made Izenberg succeed.

"I think that you need a deep grasp of history of it (boxing) to really understand it and that's something that Jerry's very good at and also obviously through in his storytelling," Matthews stated.

Sustaining relationships with sources also played a pivotal role in Jerry Izenberg's ability to write well.

For Wallace Matthews, the ultimate example was Izenberg and Ali.

"I think they each saw through the outer shell," Matthews said. "When a lot of white reporters in Jerry's day saw Ali as a braggart and a draft dodger and a symbol of everything that they were afraid of, Black Power, Muslims, something that scared the shit out of white Americans. I think Jerry saw through that, and obviously Muhammad saw past not only the color of Jerry's skin but his ethnic background and where he came from and his age, because there was a good 10-, 15-year difference in their ages as well.

"So they were two pretty unique individuals who were able to look past the obvious stereotype and see the real person, and that really helped with both of them."

"We'll never see another newspaper columnist like Jerry. In the golden age of newspapers—meaning they had money—Jerry was everywhere at every important event. He also made other events important by his presence."
-Dave Kindred

Like Jerry Izenberg, Dave Kindred closely followed boxing in its heyday. He also penned a book that captured a big slice of its history. "Sound and Fury: Two Powerful Lives, One Fateful Friendship," published in 2006, tells the intertwined story of Muhammad Ali and Howard Cosell.

This gave him a unique glimpse into Izenberg's work and his approach to his craft. After all, they saw many of the same things and experienced many of the same deadlines while visiting many of the same places for work.

"I most admire his consistency, not only in the excellence of his writing but, more important, in his world view," Kindred said in 2016. "He was and is a crusader for social justice who used his column to speak truth to power."

So how did Kindred view his relationships with Izenberg 40 years ago? And in 2016?

"I'm somewhat younger than Jerry and was awed by his reputation in the New York media world," said Kindred, a former columnist for The Sporting News, Atlanta Journal-Constitution and The Washington Post, among others. "I watched him work, read his stuff, and learned how to navigate the big time of sportswriting. Through our mutual reporting on Ali, I came to know him better but I can't call him a personal friend. He was entirely generous, still, in helping me do the book on Ali and Cosell. As I said in the intro, I think, it's a book that only three people could have done because only three people knew both those characters the way we did—Jerry, (Bob) Lipsyte, and me—and both Jerry and Bob encouraged me to take it on and helped me tremendously."

A talented wordsmith and consummate reporter, Kindred understands clearly what made Izenberg's writing unique and important.

"What Lipsyte did in bringing the real world into the sports pages, Izenberg had done first," stated Kindred without citing specific examples of Lipsyte's New York Times work. "Only later did I understand that, though. Jerry's voice—the way the column sounded, authoritative, argumentative, streetwise—was his and his alone."

Returning the focus to Ali, Kindred was asked what was special in his mind about the way Jerry wrote about Ali over the years, including numerous visits to The Greatest's training camp in Deer Lake, Pennsylvania, in the 1970s.

"Beyond Ali's cultural importance, which Jerry never let his readers forget, he had a fondness for Ali the person that he made clear in every column," Kindred said.

In conclusion, Kindred expressed great admiration for Izenberg's career.

"We'll never see another newspaper columnist like Jerry," Kindred declared. "In the golden age of newspapers—meaning they had money—Jerry was everywhere at every important event. He also made other events important by his presence. His work would serve well as a primer on sports as a piece of society in 20th century America."

"Jerry was somebody you could interview and he could talk about so many things authoritatively."
—John Dahl

The gift of gab and an eye for details that illuminate any story have carried Jerry Izenberg to great heights as a writer, commentator and broadcaster. And whenever he's a part of a discussion, Izenberg brought knowledge and wit and an ability to cut to the chase without boring anybody. He informs and gives reasoned answers, not takes.

John Dahl witnessed Jerry's endless reservoir of sports facts gleaned from decades in the business while working on ESPN's ambitious "Sports Century" project.

"Jerry was great talking about Johnny Unitas," Dahl said in 2016. "He just knows so much about so many people."

For instance, the legendary Baltimore Colts quarterback.

"The thing that I think was appealing about Jerry, why he was so sought after for repeated interviews for Sports Century was he's to the point," Dahl said. "He's authoritative. He's seen a lot. He's covered a lot. It's authentic. He's talking firsthand about these things. He's very to the point. He's opinionated in a factual sort of way.

"Jerry doesn't hold back on what he's saying, what he feels, what he experienced, and that's made him a great interview. That's what you want."

With an insider's knowledge of sports bridging the 20th and 21st centuries, Izenberg was a sought-after talking head at the end of the 1990s for the Sports Century documentary series. A who's-who of 20th century sports titans was a top-50 list that generated plenty of debate and attention.

Dahl, who oversees ESPN's "30 for 30" documentary series as part of his responsibilities as vice president and executive producer of ESPN Films and Original Content, became familiar—and impressed—with Izenberg as Sports Century came to fruition. Dahl produced eight of the top 50 greatest athlete documentaries, including on Babe Ruth and Michael Jordan.

"I crossed paths with Jerry because he became really what we called a generalist interview subject for the series and for the project because Jerry knows so much, has covered so much," Dahl related. "In the 20th century in sports, he was just a good, natural person to talk to about a lot of topics, like we would get in the early years of email and that technology as it came to be by the Sports Century project, which really launched in the summer of 1997 and started to really talk hold by the fall.

"So you think back to that time and email was really starting to kick into gear and the ability to send files and share files was huge in our ability to pull off Sports Century. So you would get an interview subject like Jerry, somebody who could talk about a lot of different topics from the greatest athletes to our other specialized shows like the most influential and the greatest games. Jerry was somebody you could interview and he could talk about so many things authoritatively, and then you'd share the transcript of that interview with the various producers and PAs (production assistants) and whatnot, we'd share transcripts with each other."

It was a wealth of valuable information.

This came to the fore when Dahl organized a panel of voters in 2005 for the "Super Bowl at 40" project.

That panel featured writers and photographers who'd cover all of the previous Super Bowls.

Since then, Dahl turned to Izenberg for vital insights for a "30 for 30" documentary on heavyweight boxers Muhammad Ali and Larry Holmes. He attended the October 1980 bout in Las Vegas.

"Again, Jerry comes through," Dahl recalled. "He's so dependable for that. He's just so good at those kinds of interviews and just getting to the point."

When Ali died in June 2016, Izenberg wrote a remarkable tribute to his friend. The column resonated with readers spanning the globe. He doesn't need validation from Twitter, but for a short period of time, the words "Jerry Izenberg" were among Twitter's top trending subjects.

"What a great piece he did. It was a firsthand account," Dahl noted. "He was talking about what he saw, the man he knew, what Ali didn't want reported. That's what makes Jerry so special.

"I never feel like Jerry's got an agenda. I just feel like he's there to speak it and write it as he saw it and sees it."

***

Former ESPN executive Mark Shapiro, the point man for the Sports Century project who now serves as the president of Endeavor, whose operations include IMG, WME and UFC, held Izenberg in high regard in his days at the sports media giant. Shapiro understood that Jerry was one of the living legends of sports media, according to Dahl.

"Jerry was in that first wave of great interviews for the project that included people like Frank Deford, Bob Lipsyte and William Nack. Bill Rhoden was in there," Dahl said, looking back.

There is no denying the fact that Izenberg is one of the giants of the business.

Or as Dahl stated with conviction: "I feel like you could put him on a Mount Rushmore of sportswriters from the 20th century. He has seen and experienced an awful lot, and he's got a good sense of humor, too. I like Jerry, I really do. I think he's terrific."

So what's his greatest attribute or strength as a journalist?

"I think his ability to personalize his experiences in a way the reader can relate to," Dahl observed. "I think the anecdotes that he shares are really valuable."

He went on: "Jerry's got a real knowledge, particularly of sports like boxing, but I think he has a real understanding of human beings. Some of his most perceptive insights have been on people that he got to know directly like Vince Lombardi and Muhammad Ali. He has a very good understanding of people and what makes them tick, so to speak."

Even in his 80s, an age when most people are retired, Izenberg consistently churned out great material in books and columns, as well as serving as an important contributor on various radio programs and documentaries. That's a remarkable legacy, Dahl said.

"I think his authority, his consistency in terms of sharing these experiences that he's had. .... Just look at his work ethic. It's why I think he's been able to endure as long as he has," Dahl pointed out. "It's incredible, it really is—what he has seen, what he has experienced. I just think his ability to really not be manipulated, but to be a voice of authority and authenticity, and to really tell it as he sees it to me is his legacy.

"That's always what made him stand out as an interview for us. There's a drama to what he says without him trying to be dramatic.

"His opinions are formed out of his experiences. The Jerry Izenberg I know doesn't just start popping off about things he doesn't know. He knows what he's talking about. There's an authority there, an expertise."

Famously, Izenberg advocated for Babe Ruth to be No. 1 on the Sports Century list, not Michael Jordan. MJ stayed at the top, but Izenberg argued his point with passion and facts.

"As a kid, he certainly was aware of the regard and how (Ruth) was written about and talked about when he was growing up. Yeah, I can appreciate Jerry's opinion on that," Dahl recounted.

"Yeah, I understand Jerry's opinion on that. When you go back and look at what Ruth did to transform baseball. That's where he was as a pitcher and then he completely changed the game as a hitter, and everybody says the Babe Ruth of this, the Babe Ruth of that, I think Jerry was probably looking at it saying, 'Well then why don't we just go with Babe Ruth?' So I can understand why he thought the voters should've ultimately selected Ruth."

Dahl understands what makes a story compelling and said he considers Izenberg's life a natural subject for a documentary. He cited the careers of longtime Sports Illustrated photographer Neil Leifer and the late Dick Schaap, the seemingly omnipresent journalist, author and broadcaster, as examples.

Izenberg's Super Bowl streak, which stretched from 1967 to 2019, is a defining trait of his career. And how many of us do anything noteworthy 50-plus years in a row?

"Wow, that is extremely impressive," Dahl said. "Every single Super Bowl, that says it all about Jerry."

"His Ali obit was the only one I read, because I knew it was the only one I'd have to read."
-Tim Brown

You can't always appreciate a person's professional accomplishments or standards right away when you meet them. Sometimes, it takes years, maybe decades, to do so.

Which was the case for Tim Brown, now an MLB columnist for Yahoo Sports, when he looks back on his impressions of Jerry Izenberg from more than two decades ago.

"I grew up in White Plains (New York) reading the New York tabs and recall being very excited when The New York Times jumped both feet into sports with a Monday section called, cleverly, SportsMonday," Brown said. "Anyway, those were my guys, the New York guys, and by the time I'd returned to the area in 1997 to cover the Yankees for The Star-Ledger I remained largely unfamiliar with Jerry Izenberg, from the Jersey paper, pre-Internet. I knew the name. I knew the reputation. But there weren't a lot of Star-Ledgers lying around the lobby of the Grand Hyatt or even on the corner newsstands.

"What I learned upon being hired by The Star-Ledger was the man was god-like in that newsroom, a seen-it-all, done-it-all, captured-it-all reporter, writer, columnist and the soul of a great newspaper that hadn't yet begun slipping away."

And here's how Brown remembers their first encounter:

"The '98 Yankees began the season on the road, seven games through Anaheim, Oakland and Seattle. They lost their first three, and arrived at Yankee Stadium for their home opener on a chilly Friday afternoon a clumsy 3-4. I sat in the press box mid-morning, eager to get through the ceremony of that game and into the weekend, my first days off in a couple of months. There was movement to my right.

"Hi, Jerry Izenberg," the man said, holding out his hand.

"Tim," I said. "New guy."

"Then we sat through four hours of an awful game the Yankees would win, 17-13 (against the Athletics).

This seemed to displease Jerry very much, four hours of 32 hits and 30 runs. And when it was over, and he'd written his column, and a day game had leaked into a hellish commute out of the city and back to Jersey on a Friday night, Jerry dropped his computer into his bag and said, 'Well, see you in October.'

"And it was true. I did not see him again until the playoffs."

But that doesn't diminish Brown's profound respect for Jerry's work.

"I came to Jerry's work late and spoke to him only occasionally," he admitted. "Indeed, I guess I can speak to the fact Jerry was both an industry giant and an industry secret. I was a huge fan of Red Smith, of Jim Murray, of the old New York columnists, and yet it took a couple years in Jersey to learn about Jerry, to understand exactly who he was and why he was it, to circle back on columns I wish I'd read in the moment.

"What I discovered was a newspaperman, a reporter, a journalist, a columnist who stood alongside the iconic sportswriters of the past century. He wrote with composure and dignity. He told his stories and took his stands without screaming and falling all over himself. He did not write pop-up columns lined with knee-jerk opinions. His career told a story, end to end, and some of it was his story, but most of it was the story of our world, how we saw it or—better—how we would come to see it."

Brown concluded by sharing these thoughts: "I should've been paying better attention to Jerry, and I think I speak for much of the country's sports fans when I say so. Now I go back and it's like reading a history book, and I mean that as a compliment. His Ali obit was the only one I read, because I knew it was the only one I'd have to read, and it was glorious. That's about the best I can say about a fellow writer. That, and I wish he'd keep writing forever."

"If I ever actually agree to a book, Jerry, I want you to be the one to write it," Pete Rozelle once told Jerry Izenberg.
—Joe Browne

Jerry Izenberg and Joe Browne go way back.

They both attended the Ice Bowl on Dec. 31, 1967, in Green Bay, Wisconsin. Vince Lombardi's Packers vs. Tom Landry's Cowboys at Lambeau Field.

And more than 50 years later, even the run-up to that event remains an unforgettable experience for Browne.

"I had a rough intro to him," Browne recalled. "We both were at the Ice Bowl in Green Bay. I was working part time while I was in college and happened to be at the airport when Jerry arrived. I recognized him from his photo in the paper and asked him if he and another writer wanted a ride to downtown Green Bay. He sat in the front passenger seat and thought I was driving too fast on the snowy roads. He asked me how long I had been driving.

"I told him I had just passed my driver's test earlier that month on Dec. 7. He said, 'That figures. Pearl Harbor Day. Try not to get us killed before you get us to the hotel.' "

Decades later, they can joke about that incident. Browne can also provide authoritative insights about Izenberg's career.

"When you opened the paper in the morning, you never were sure what Jerry had in store," observed longtime PR man Browne, who began working for the NFL as a teenage intern in 1965 and served in a number of high-level positions before retiring in March 2016. At the time, Browne was the league's longest-serving office employee.

Browne added: "It could be a well-reasoned, heavy-duty criticism of some phase of our league operation or it might be an emotional column on some high school athlete—raised in a single-parent family in Newark—who was overcoming major obstacles to succeed."

Did Browne and former NFL commissioner Pete Rozelle, who passed away in 1996, have a cordial relationship with Izenberg?

"Pete really enjoyed Jerry and appreciated his journalism style," said Browne. "Jerry talked decades ago to Pete about a book on his life.

"Pete was very hesitant but threw Jerry the consolation: 'If I ever actually agree to a book, Jerry, I want you to be the one to write it.' I am very pleased that Jerry was able to complete the book, which he began many many years ago."

"Rozelle: A Biography" was published in November 2014. David Stern, the longtime NBA commissioner, wrote the foreword. In wrapping up the foreword, Stern penned these words: *"There is nobody better able to tell Pete's story than the acclaimed journalist and columnist Jerry Izenberg. Jerry has reported on many of the key sports figures and events of the past sixty years. He is one of only a handful of reporters to have covered every Super Bowl, and few people, if any, are as knowledgeable about the sport of football and the NFL as he. As one of the most highly respected professionals in his field, Jerry's body of work is extraordinary and his knowledge of the subject unparalleled..."*

Based on his decades of service to the NFL, Browne is uniquely qualified to provide an intelligent assessment of Izenberg's coverage of the league and his role as a pundit behind the camera.

"Steve Sabol, the creative genius behind NFL Films, loved Jerry because not only does he have a fantastic long-term memory but he is not shy about expressing himself in front of the camera," Brown said. "(George) Halas, Lombardi, Paul Brown, Tom Landry ... he knew and dealt with them all and has a story about each one."

For decades, there were big-time columnists at the big papers—Red Smith, Jim Murray, Shirley Povich to name a few—who covered all the big events. Nowadays, there are many more specialists working for online sites, NFL.com and the shrinking number of newspapers.

So what has made Izenberg particularly unique, not just for his football columns, but for his overall work at The Star-Ledger?

"When we celebrated the 50th anniversary of the Super Bowl in February 2016, I hosted a panel of fans and media who had attended every game," Brown recounted. "Jerry with his terrific stories was the second-most popular panelist. The only one better was Norma Hunt, who as Pro Football Hall of Famer Lamar Hunt's widow is the only woman in the world to have attended every Super Bowl. Norma's storytelling style is a little different that Jerry's but they were both great."

There were mixed perceptions of Izenberg at NFL headquarters, according to Browne.

"The league office personnel were split on Jerry," he said. "Pete Rozelle and the PR department appreciated his tremendous clout not just with his readers but also his impact on other media covering the league. Others in the office who didn't know him as we did thought he was a little odd. Wearing a cowboy hat in August in the middle of Manhattan as Jerry does can have that effect on some folks.

"I think next to Rozelle the closest friend Jerry had in our office was Buddy Young, who was a 5-foot-5 former college and pro scat back who Pete hired to help players get jobs in the offseason. Jerry and Buddy had many late-night conversations. However if you ever transcribed them the next day, I don't think too many of them dealt with on-the-field football activities."

Throughout his decades as a columnist, no institution was off limits for Izenberg. This was true even during times of celebration, such as in the days before Super Bowl 50, when he advocated for the league to honor Rozelle at that time.

The headline: "Two words that should have been spoken at the Super Bowl: Pete Rozelle."

"There is no mistaking when Jerry takes a stand or has an opinion," Browne said, reacting to the column about Rozelle. "He makes it very clear what he believes."

Browne also recognizes what many others who've followed Izenberg's career have noted: He didn't have the biggest national platform, which limited his exposure to some extent.

"I believe he would be much more appreciated nationally if he had decided to write for The New York Times than The Star-Ledger," Browne concluded. "However, he loved his Jersey paper and wouldn't move."

"Izenberg has a gift for painting characters. If you never saw Sonny Liston or Bart Starr perform, he brings them to life."
-Bijan Bayne

A studious observer, Bijan Bayne pays attention to the hallmarks of culture and the titans of American sports. He's also noticed how important Jerry Izenberg's work has been in chronicling changes in sports over the past half century.

Asked what are the first things that come to mind when reflecting on Izenberg's career, Bayne offered this viewpoint: "The fact that he has a firmer grasp on the cultural and social changes of 1960s sport than anyone alive, even (Bob) Lipsyte. He is the last storyteller from a breed of (George) Plimpton and (Dick) Schaap. He truly 'got' Muhammad Ali, which is no given."

An author, critic and sports historian whose books include "Elgin Baylor: The Man Who Changed Basketball," Bayne believes Izenberg has natural talent to provide a broader context and perspective to his writings.

Izenberg's writing trademarks are "his recall for the backdrop of the times, and his ability to frame sport as a microcosm of society, without judging," Bayne stated.

Which is why his legacy in sports journalism is immense, according to Bayne.

"Izenberg is vital to any fan, media or historian seeking perspective on how figures such as (Willie) Mays, (Mickey) Mantle, Ali and (Vince) Lombardi helped shape the culture," he said.

And what are two or three traits of Jerry's traits that shine through in his columns and interviews?

"Izenberg has a gift for painting characters. If you never saw Sonny Liston or Bart Starr perform, he brings them to life. If you did, he gets to their depth as a novelist would," Bayne noted.

Bayne insisted that Jerry's work in documenting Ali and the overall landscape of boxing was "invaluable."

"He was at the venues," Bayne said, "and knew the opposition, both inside and outside the ring, in real time. He saw the U.S. change, slowly..."

As a writer and broadcaster, Izenberg used college football as a backdrop to educate the public about the sport in the Deep South at a historically black college, Grambling. The significance of this work resonates with Bayne.

"He and Howard Cosell played a large role in introducing Grambling football to mainstream audiences, and it was vivid," Bayne noted, citing Izenberg's True magazine feature "A Whistle-Stop School with Big-Time Talent" about coach Eddie Robinson's school was chosen as one of 1967's entries in the year's Best Sports Stories anthology.

Bayne revealed that the Grambling feature remains his favorite piece from Izenberg's large vault of writings.

"I enjoy his work about Ali, but 'A Whistle-Stop School with Big-Time Talent' captures both the reporter and the creative writer," Bayne said.

In conclusion, Bayne was asked for his viewpoint about whether Jerry's work has been overlooked by a lot of the general public because he wasn't at The New York Times, New York Post, New York Daily News, The Washington Post or other big media outlets with high-profile websites?

"Yes, the Newark byline has perhaps (not with media) precluded his inclusion with Jim Murray, Lipsyte, Schaap, Bill Nack, Edwin Pope, Furman Bisher and Dan Jenkins," Bayne concluded. "But it makes Jerry 'Jerry.'"

"Jerry can bring a vast historical knowledge to the Derby, as he covered it during a time that most of us in the press box were in diapers or in grade school."
-Gene Kershner

In this era of shrinking newsrooms, Gene Kershner of The Buffalo News is one of a select few who specializes in horse racing coverage. His work has introduced him to Jerry Izenberg. They formed a friendship in recent years.

"I formally met Jerry for the first time at the 2015 Breeders' Cup at Keeneland during American Pharoah's Triple Crown year," Kershner recalled. "Jerry sat across from me wearing his patented cowboy hat that he would be known to wear. I knew of Jerry, of course, from his coverage of many Super Bowls and (Kentucky) Derbies.

"The Buffalo News' Larry Felser was one of (only a few) gentlemen that covered all of the first 37 Super Bowls through his retirement. ... We chatted about his relationship with the late Mr. Felser and his Super Bowl streak.

"During the two days we exchanged pleasantries and he from time to time would ask me a question. After we both finished writing about American Pharoah's historic win, he asked me to help him to the media bus to make sure he would get back to the hotel where his wife was waiting for him. I escorted him down and there was still a lot of traffic between us and the hotel, as Keeneland (Racecourse in Lexington, Kentucky) is a difficult place to exit and it was the first time they had a crowd the size of 50,000 for the Breeders' Cup."

Providing assistance to Izenberg gave Kershner a chance to gain a greater appreciation for his colleague's life.

"He needed some help getting to the press shuttle so I volunteered my services," Kershner remembered.

"Over the next hour the 85-year-old regaled me with stories of Muhammad Ali, Secretariat, Rozelle (his 13th book), Rutgers football (not really) and Bill Belichick."

Fast forward to 2017, a few days after Izenberg covered his 51st Kentucky Derby. Kershner was asked what that fact means to him and how Jerry has used the knowledge he gained across the decades for his columns.

"Jerry can bring a vast historical knowledge to the Derby, as he covered it during a time that most of us in the press box were in diapers or in grade school," Kershner said. "The references to the past and how he can bring (and) assimilate past Derbies to the present makes his columns a must-read, before and after every Run for the Roses."

And how has Jerry, throughout his 80s, gained and maintained rapport with longtime sources such as owners, trainers and jockeys and newer contacts?

"At Keeneland, he would still make his way back to the barns to talk to the trainers, which is amazing," Kershner noted.

To this day, Kershner insists that Izenberg's Derby work is always must-read material.

"I always read his writings before the Derby to remind me of the creativity that's required to succeed in telling a story that a whole room full of writers are trying to tell," Kershner commented. "I'll also read his post-race commentary and inevitably there is something he picked up on that no one else, even the daily beat turf writers missed."

A knack for finding the most interesting details and nuggets of information shine through in Jerry's work.

What else stands out about his personality? Kershner was asked.

"(He's) creative, spontaneous, spunky, eloquent, funny," Kershner offered.

Acknowledgments

Jerry Izenberg has lived a remarkable life, and it 's a blessing to share his stories and his insights with readers. I and humbled and honored to share them with you. Furthermore, I am forever grateful to have had the the opportunity to listen to Jerry's stories and learn a few things about his life and career. Thank you, Jerry.

Boxing publicist Fred Sternburg played a pivotal role in opening my eyes to the vast network of writers and broadcasters who are aware and in awe of Jerry's talents. Thank you, Fred, for sharing generous portions of your email Rolodex. You have provided tremendous assistance.

Friends and family also encouraged me to pursue this project. I am extremely thankful for your words of inspiration.

Journalism colleagues and acquaintances also provided support. Readers who've followed my career also checked in from time to time and kept asking when I would be done with this book. Their inquiries motivated me to keep going.

I am also humbled by the opportunity to interact with several dozen individuals from the sports media world and beyond, including Jerry Green, Ira Berkow, Jeremy Schaap, Bob and Rick Wolff, John Schulian, Wallace Matthews, Dave Kindred, John Dahl, Tim Brown, Joe Browne, Bijon Bayne, Gene Kershner, Jim Lampley, Sherry Ross, Alex Belth, Bill Dwyre, George Solomon, Dick Weiss, Peter Vecsey, Dave Goren, Christine Brennan, Wayne Coffey, Robert Lipsyte, Ivan Maisel, Kevin Iole, John McClain, Greg Bishop, George Vecsey, Charley Steiner, Cormac Gordon, Tom Verducci, Michael Socolow, James Fiorentino, Richard Lapchick, Thomas Gerbasi, Neil Best, Patrick Farabaugh, Filip Bondy, Bob Papa, Dave Sims, Pat Borzi and Keith Olbermann. Thomas Hauser's expertise also proved invaluable.

And a big shout out to the chancellor at Izenberg's alma mater, Rutgers University-Newark, Nancy Cantor, for her insights, too.

To everyone interviewed for this book, thank you for your detailed and short answers to my questions. I truly appreciate your ideas.

Izenberg's contemporaries Edwin Pope and Dave Anderson, the latter of whom figures prominently in this project, passed away before the book was completed. I wish they were still here to see the finished product, and I wanted to thank them again for their time and generosity. I express the same sentiments for well-respected NBA writer Marty McNeal, who held Jerry in high regard. McNeal died earlier this year.

Don't miss out!

Visit the website below and you can sign up to receive emails whenever Ed Odeven publishes a new book. There's no charge and no obligation.

https://books2read.com/r/B-A-GEZL-KWQIB

BOOKS 2 READ

Connecting independent readers to independent writers.

About the Author

Ed Odeven is a veteran sportswriter based in Tokyo. Currently writing for *JAPAN Forward*, he spent nearly 14 years at *The Japan Times*. Odeven, who reported from the 2008 Beijing Olympics and 2012 London Games, served as the sports editor for Arizona State University's *State Press* and the *Arizona Daily Sun*.

Read more at www.edodevenreporting.com.

Made in the USA
Las Vegas, NV
13 June 2021